HOW THINGS WORK ?

HOW THINGS WORK ?

K. Krishna Murty

PUSTAK MAHAL®

Publishers
Pustak Mahal®

Administrative office and sale centre

J-3/16 , Daryaganj, New Delhi-110002
☎ 23276539, 23272783, 23272784 • *Fax:* 011-23260518
E-mail: info@pustakmahal.com • *Website:* www.pustakmahal.com

Branches
Bengaluru: ☎ 080-22234025 • *Telefax:* 080-22240209
E-mail: pustak@airtelmail.in • pustak@sancharnet.in
Mumbai: ☎ 022-22010941, 022-22053387
E-mail: rapidex@bom5.vsnl.net.in
Patna: ☎ 0612-3294193 • *Telefax:* 0612-2302719
E-mail: rapidexptn@rediffmail.com

ISBN 978-81-223-1482-3

Edition 2016

Printed at : Radha Offset, Delhi

Dedication

I walked behind my barefoot father
My mother loves my books (she can't read)

Index

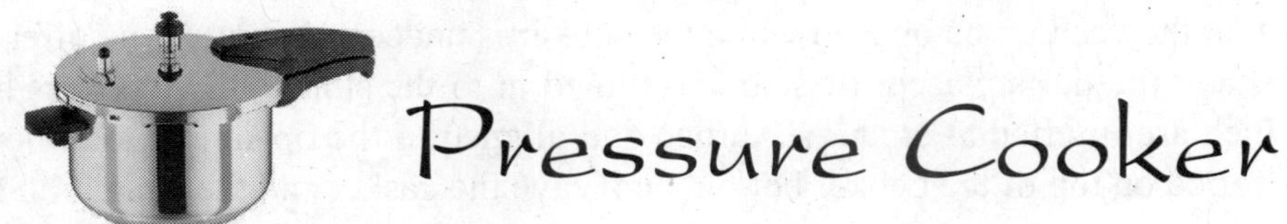

Pressure Cooker

Walk into any Indian kitchen – you will find cookers of all sizes and shapes, made of aluminium, or stainless steel. They can easily cook idly and daal in a jiffy and treat you with almost all curries. They cook in shortest time and provide healthy meals too! As the food is cooked above the normal boiling point of water, most micro-organisms are killed. These cookers hiss, they whistle or they pop steam up! Badly treated they can blow up and paint a modern art of half cooked vegetables, rice, etc., on the walls and roof. That's the Pressure Cooker.

We know that water boils at 100°C, well, of course at sea level[1] . You may continue to heat, but the temperature stays the same. That's the normal open vessel cooking. The cooking takes longer and longer as the temperature would not rise. Then that's also the best way to destroy vitamins, particularly vitamin C, and B and other nutrients. Experts recommend as little water as possible and rapid cooking, because excess water washes away the nutrients and heat spoils them.

On the other hand, go up a hill station say 2000 or 3000 meters above say level[2] , water boils much lower than 100°C, so cooking takes much longer and even some foods cannot be cooked at all in open vessels.

So what to do? The solution – Pressure cooker! Simple science tells us that if we can raise steam pressure, temperature also will rise, but reverse also happens. So put an absolutely tight lid on the vessel; let no steam escape. Continue to heat, both the pressure and temperature inside the vessel will rise[3] . Food is cooked by the high temperatures inside the cooker. That is what a pressure cooker does! And nutrients stay within.

Most pressure cookers are designed to cook at about 1kg/cm^2 and 120°C. That's high temperature and pressure of steam which can easily scald human body. So, a good number of safety features are built into the modern pressure cookers[4]. A rubber or silicone gasket prevents steam from leaking out. A weight valve or regulator controls pressure build up. If this is blocked or fails to work, a

1 A little science; Atmospheric pressure has profound effect on us. Atmosphere exerts about one kg of pressure on every square centimetre. Sea level is taken as standard and water boils at 100°C. As we go uphill, this pressure reduces, so does the boiling point of water.

2 At about 1000 meters, water boils at 96°C, at about 2000 mtrs, water boils at 93°C, and at about 3000 mtrs, water boils at 90°C. This phenomenon is generally used in evaporation in process industries.

3 As the pressure rises, the boiling point of water also raises. At 0.5 kg pressure more at every square centimeter (0.5kg/cm^2) water boils at 115°C and at 1kg/cm^2 water boils at 120°C. That's the trick of pressure cooker.

4 Initially, people were reluctant to use them. The term... 'In a pressure cooker', implied disaster.

safety valve releases pressure. Some models also feature gasket release system which opens up the gasket and allow the steam to escape reducing the pressure. Cooker lids are designed with double lock safety so that they cannot be opened while the cooker is under pressure. Some offer bayonet-style locking where the lid is placed, twisted and turned in to the slots. Other cookers have oval shaped lids which are inserted at an angle, turned and aligned to the opening. Good housewives keep the lid inverted on top of the cooker bottom and leave the gasket and the weight on the lid.

Generations Of Cookers: In 1679, the French mathematician and physicist Denis Papin invented the first pressure cooker, calling it a steam digester. Unfortunately, it exploded during a demonstration at the Royal Society. He returned soon after with a safety valve invented for it. His invention cooked meat quicker and bones softened. He cooked a meal for the Royal Society and King Charles II[5].

In 1938 Alfred Vischler patented his 'Flex-Seal Speed Cooker.' The world's first commercial pressure cooker made by National Presto Industries was exhibited at the New York World's Fair in 1939[6].

Often made of aluminium and sometimes with stainless steel, cookers are generally used on top of the stove but there are also electrical models and microwave models.

The older design has been in use for 100 years, but still popular. Most first-generation pressure cookers use a pressure of about 1 kg/cm^2 or less, with a weight to release pressure. In the fixed weight pressure regulators, weights are more or less permanently attached to the vent pipe, they just rise up a little bit when the cooker is fully pressurized. In the more popular version the weight can be easily removed for cleaning. Another variation popular in India is the pressure cooker which makes a whistle as if they are tailor made for Indian cookery. Second generation cookers are sleek and quiet with a spring-loaded valve, designed not to release any steam during operation.

Pressure Release: The higher temperature causes the food to cook faster; almost reduced to 1/3 conventional cooking times, flavours and nutrients are not lost into thin air. The actual cooking time also depends on the recipe and pressure release method. Ladies pour water on the cooker, lift the weight with a spoon or just wait until the cooker lid can be opened depending on the time they have on hand and of course the recipe.

Parts and Features

Pressure Regulator / Vent Valve: The pressure regulator/vent weight/vent valve is an accurately weighted device which regulates the operating pressure. It lifts up at the exact time when the cooker reaches 1 kg/cm^2. Never place anything over the pressure regulator/vent weight while cooking. Never allow the vent tube to get clogged. Burnt food, even traces of food and scaling can block

5 By watching the safety valve move up and down, Papin conceived of the idea of a piston and cylinder engine, but did not follow up. In 1697, engineer Thomas Savery built the first commercial steam engine.

6 In the early days of pressure cookers, people thought pressure cooking was witchcraft. Continuous hissing added to the lore. They thought of the same about movies.

the vent pipe and weight valve may fail. Remove the weight from your pressure cooker; clean the inside hole using a small brush or cotton swab or piece of cloth in a see-saw manner. If the weight needs to be replaced, replace one with the original model from an authorized dealer only. Pressure regulator weights are not interchangeable.

Gaskets: Gaskets are made of silicone rubber or other polymers as they make better sealing and do not retain food odours. Don't pull or stretch the gasket because you'll really stretch it forever. Always remove the gasket after every use and wash it. Store it loosely in the lid or the base. Heat and misuse, not age, will eventually reduce its life. Unfortunately, they won't give any advance warning, follows Murphy's Law faithfully and fail at the most inopportune time.

If the cooker does not come to pressure normally or the steam leaks out around the lid, it's time to change the gasket. Similarly, if the gasket does not seat in the groove or the lid is hard to open and close, it's time to replace the gasket.

Do not let your cooker run dry as heat shortens the life of the gasket material. Prolonged exposure to heat or high heat can actually melt the gasket which would then stick to the seating.

Care and Tips

While I do not wish this chapter to form a cookery book, some tips would be in order.

✓ Never cook when you are under pressure: that's the first law of cooking, more so with pressure cooking!

✓ Never heat the cooker without water.

✓ Do not fill the unit over 2/3 full. When cooking dal /pulses which sprout, never fill the cooker more than 1/3 full. Over filling may clog the steam vent and develop excess pressure.

Problems and Solutions

☹ Cooker not building up pressure

1. Not enough water or cooking liquid - Follow the recipe for the correct amount of water.
2. Not closed properly.
3. Not enough heat - Always heat it over high flame and reduce after the pressure is reached.
4. Dirty or obstructed cooker valve.

5. Improper positioning of gasket and/or lid.
6. Dirty or warped cooker gasket, seating or lid.
7. Hardened gasket.
8. Pressure cooker is overfilled. Never fill it more than two-thirds full.

☹ **Steam leaks around the lid though the gasket is new:** It looks like a bad gasket case but often the problem lies in the lid. Aluminium being a softer metal than stainless steel is more prone to warping. Age, overheating and use of excessive force while opening a pressurised lid are some of the causes. Angry housewife may bang it, drop it and throw it or a short housewife may use it as a stool. This may create tiny bit of distortion which would be difficult to detect but the cooker leaks either there or around. The same can happen if the seating is cleaned with rough instruments like screw drivers or scrappers, sand paper and abrasives. Only recourse would be replacement.

Finally what's cooking today?

Gas Stove

Look at the face of a modern housewife when her gas cylinder empties out. No warning, no indication. Children getting ready for school, time up for husband's office. She is a worried lot! Her little comfort and precious time are lost. Nothing better improved her kitchen convenience than the advent of gas cooking[7].

Gas in the gas cylinder is actually liquid. It is liquefied petroleum gas (LPG) which is a mixture of butane and propane. It is gas at normal temperature and atmospheric pressure. However, for the convenience in handling, transportation and storage, it is converted into liquid form by the application of moderate pressure. So what comes out at the burner head is highly inflammable gas, which can be ignited with a match-stick or lighter. This liquefied petroleum gas is very economical boasting high heat output calorific value of 11,900 kcal/kg. LPG is a clean fuel which does not create soot on the cooking vessels also efficient and environmentally friendly. It is colourless and odourless as well, but to make it easily detectable when leaking, a compound called Mercaptan sulphur is added so that it gives out a foul smell.

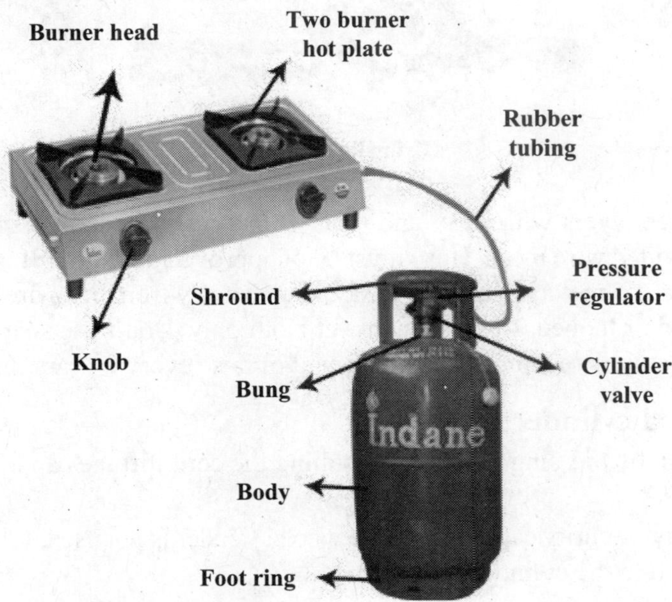

7 In 1913, Dr. Walter Snelling was granted a patent for his method of producing LP gases.

It is safer than most other conventional fuels, as long as you follow the simple and basic rules. LPG ignites only within the specified LPG- Air ratio of 2% to 9%, not more, not less. Petrol has an ignition temperature of 257°C whereas propane has a higher ignition temperature, about 450-510°C which makes it less likely to ignite spontaneously. The gas itself is twice heavier than air and so it tends to settle at lower levels. So, adequate ground level ventilation is required where LPG is stored. LPG would float as it is lighter than water.

For Domestic use, the gas comes in cylinders of 14.2 kg, while heavier cylinders of 19 kg and 47.5 kg cylinders are meant exclusively for commercial and industrial use. These cylinders are manufactured by special techniques by the approved manufacturers and are spray painted with a signal red colour. Do not accept the cylinder if the seal is broken.

The older gas stoves were made from cast iron but presently one can buy cookers with stainless steel body. Stove has common line connected to a LPG hose. The common line has valves for opening or closing gas to individual burners, with mixing lines leading to the burners.

Gas cylinder has a valve fixed on it which is normally closed. A pressure regulator sits on it. When it is opened, it reduces and regulates the pressure of the gas coming out of the cylinder. Gas enters the stove through a flexible hose, and the burner valve controls the flow. The gas goes through a mixing line where it vaporises and also sucks air due to venturi action for effective burning. Gas air mixture burns at the burner end. Good gas stoves have high thermal efficiency of about 68%. Use of small burner in a LPG stove saves fuel.

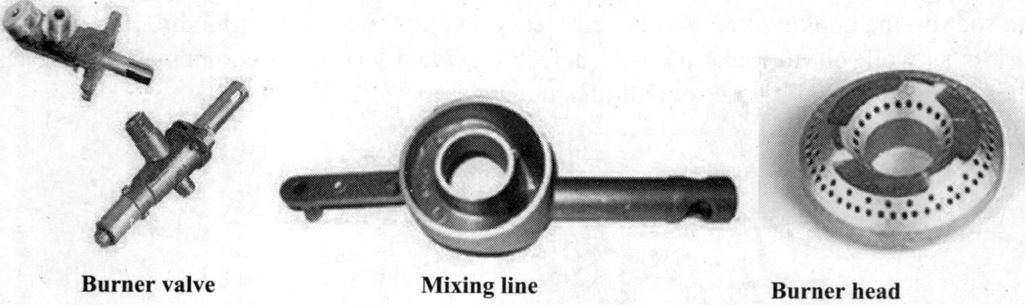

Burner valve **Mixing line** **Burner head**

Good LPG hose has three layers with inner and outer layers made of special quality rubber and middle layer made of braided wire mesh. Hose must be of approved quality, (ISI mark) and as short as possible, not more than 1.5 meters. Needless to say, keep it away from heat, fire and spillages and without getting it twisted or looped. Clean it with wet cloth only. Don't use soap to push the tube over the nozzle. Manufacturers recommend replacement of hose every 2 years if not earlier.

Connecting the filled cylinder

- ✓ Remove the safety cap by pressing it down. By pulling the cord, lift the cap off the valve of the cylinder.
- ✓ Always keep the safety/ security cap on the valve when cylinder is not used, full or empty. When using the cylinder tie it to the cylinder.

- ✓ Check whether sealing ring is in place inside the cylinder valve by feeling the same with the help of your little finger. Do not use the cylinder if the ring is missing or found damaged, as the gas will surely leak. Put the safety cap back and return the cylinder.
- ✓ To mount the regulator on the filled cylinder, keep the regulator in the OFF position.

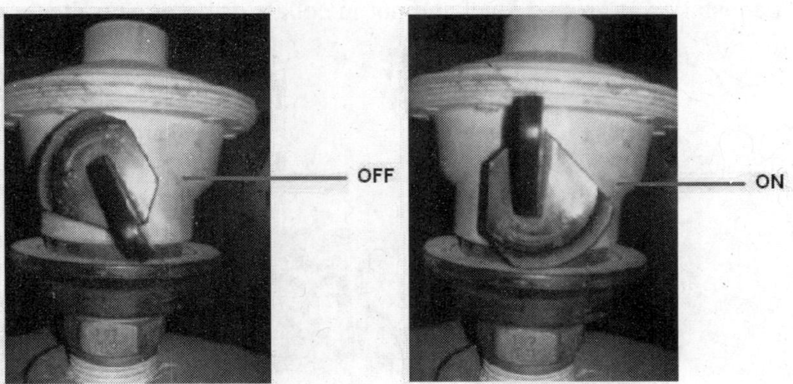

- ✓ Grip the regulator and pull up the plastic bush.
- ✓ Place the regulator vertically on the valve and press it down till its edge touches the hexagon of the valve on the cylinder with a gentle swivel.
- ✓ Release the black plastic bush and then press it down.(You may hear click sound)

Disconnecting the empty cylinder

- ✓ Turn the switch knob of the regulator from ON position to OFF position.
- ✓ Grip the regulator and pull the bush (black plastic locking ring) up and lift the regulator by giving a gentle swivel.
- ✓ Regulator will then get detached from the valve on the cylinder.

IF YOU SMELL GAS.

- ✓ Do not operate electrical switches.
- ✓ Ensure that stove knobs are in OFF position.
- ✓ Do not light a matchstick just to detect the leakage of LPG.
- ✓ Switch OFF the regulator by turning the knob clockwise to the OFF position.
- ✓ Open all doors and windows.
- ✓ If the smell persists, call your nearest emergency service cell.
- ✓ Safety is of primary importance in all cooking, particularly in gas cooking.
- ✓ Do not wear nylon garments or loose fabrics when cooking.
- ✓ Do not place the gas stove near a window. Strong wind may put off the flame causing accumulation of LPG in the room.
- ✓ Do not use long curtains on windows near your stove. Gentle breeze can blow them over the burner and catch fire.
- ✓ Never leave the cooking appliance unattended when in use. Keep the regulator in OFF position after cooking is over or during night.

- ✓ No DIY (DO IT YOURSELF) repairs on gas stoves. Call an authorized mechanic.
- ✓ Clean the burners regularly.
- ✓ Always keep the cylinders in a vertical position with the valve on top. If cylinder is placed in any other position, liquid LPG may flow out.
- ✓ Cylinders must be installed at ground level and not in cellars or basements etc.

- ✓ Keep in such a way that cylinder, rubber tube, and pressure regulators knob are easily accessible.
- ✓ Avoid keeping puja lamp and refrigerator in the kitchen.
- ✓ Cylinders must not be installed close to any other heating appliance or combustible articles like kerosene, petrol, etc.
- ✓ Gas stove must always be at a suitable height, never on the floor. Do not use a wooden top table.
- ✓ Do not keep any shelves or spoon racks on the wall near the stove. We have a tendency to lean over to pick up something from there.
- ✓ The room/ kitchen should be well ventilated. Do not ever shut the windows and doors.
- ✓ Do not use cylinder as a storage space for any utensil or cloth etc.
- ✓ Check your cylinder at the time of receipt and regularly by applying soap solution on cylinder joints. The appearance of soap bubbles indicates leak points. Do not use open flame to detect leaks.

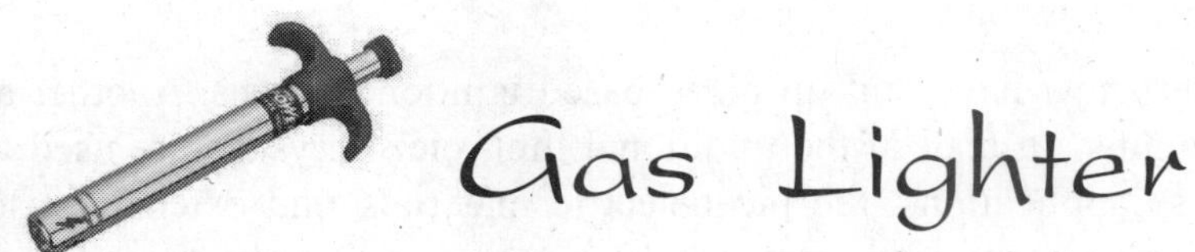

Gas Lighter

When the Neanderthal man took two stones and rubbed them, there came a spark. The civilisation began. He used this spark to light fire and cook his hunting. It was the first step towards man's progress and prosperity, from cooking our dinner to sending spacecrafts to the Mars. That brings us to the kitchen, where we have one more indispensable tool, just to light that spark.

Interestingly the original spark for this small little gadget came from Jacques Curie and Pierre Curie in 1880-81. It is the ubiquitous gas lighter in every kitchen with a LPG stove. *Ever wonder that a small force of thumb can produce a spark of one thousand volts?*

Operation: What you see outside is a button in a gas lighter. A little hammer and spring are attached to this button. On the other end of the lighter is a piezo-ceramic crystal. When this button is pressed, first the hammer is moved away from the crystal. When the button is pressed beyond a limit, the spring releases the hammer. Soon the hammer hits the crystal and a high voltage of around 800 volts is generated[8]. This voltage is applied across small air gap between two metallic points. When the high voltage jumps across the contact points, a spark is produced. The spark ignites the liquid petroleum gas to produce flame. In gas lighters 'lead zirconate titanate' (PZT) crystals are used due to their low cost and high sensitivity.

The picture shows the ignition head containing a thin metal rod around a plastic casing. A spark is produced at the corner of this metal piece; interestingly the spark is not produced at the same place each time.

Care and Tips

- ✓ After each use keep the lighter at a safe place.
- ✓ Keep the lighter always clean.
- ✓ If grease, oil or food particles accumulate around, the spark may not generate.

8 Certain materials known as piezoelectric crystals when subjected to mechanical stress produce an electric field and vice versa. The degree of electric field produced is directly proportional to the magnitude of force applied. This principle is termed as piezoelectricity and the crystals such as Tourmaline and quartz which exhibit such property are called piezo-electric crystals.

✓ If the spark does not occur, try cleaning around with damp cloth. Use only after dry. If the spark still does not occur, buy a new one.

Many types of gas burners now have built-in piezo-based ignition systems. Another application is the electric cigarette lighter. Instead of the traditional flint, piezo crystals are used to give out a spark. Apart from these applications, the piezoelectric materials find extensive use in many other technological applications requiring extremely high precision like ultrasonic transducers for medical imaging and also industrial non-destructive testing (NDT). There are other interesting applications like:

- Piezoelectric beepers in everything electronic nowadays
- Piezoelectric tweeters in stereo speakers
- Sound-generating arrays for sonar, fish finders and ultrasound devices
- Quartz crystals used in computers and digital clocks, etc.

A precursor to this is the flint stone lighter, or the common cigarette lighter. A spark is created by striking metal against a flint[9]. As the lighter wheel is turned, it strikes a flint stone making a spark but also opens the valve, on the small little tank containing Naphtha or Petrol, sometimes even LP gas. Vapours coming out of the valve are ignited.

Piezoelectric materials also work the other way – if you apply a voltage across the crystal, the crystal will change shape. If the voltage varies the shape also varies, enough to drive small speakers. There goes the beeper, a little piezoelectric speaker.

Here is the picture of a very common piezo buzzer which operates on DC. Actual transducer or the piezo element is shown on the left. It is encapsulated in a cylindrical plastic housing shown in the middle, which also acts as a resonator to improve the sound and sound quality. A hole on the top propagates the sound. The structure is shown in the right hand picture.

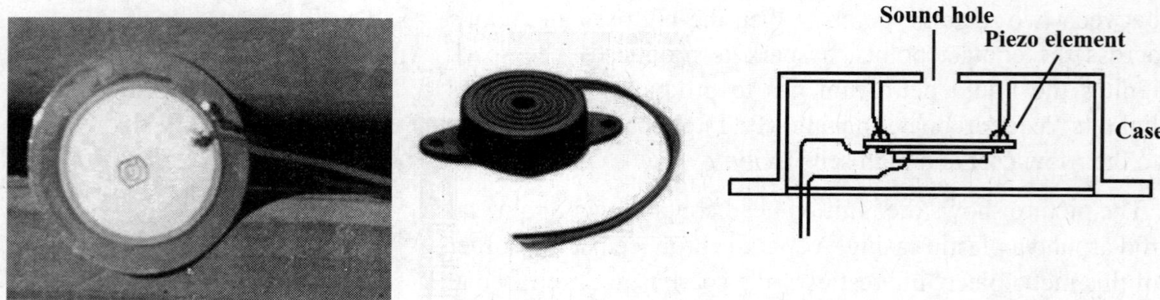

9 Carl Auer von Welsbach patented ferrocerium (often misidentified as flint) in 1903. When scratched, it produced a large spark. Using Carl Auer von Welsbach's flint, companies like Ronson were able to develop practical and easy to use lighters.

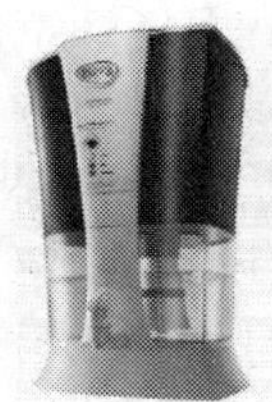

Purify Water

In my childhood, I used to look with awe and wonder at the three pots kept in the railway stations as the water dripped from one pot to the bottom pot. I loved to take cool and clean water there. I used to stand behind my mother and watch her filtering water with a simple cloth tied around the mouth of a vessel. Alas! Good old days and simple ways are gone! Today water purification has become a bare necessity. Depleting water resources, erratic monsoon cycles, industrial wastes, fresh contaminants, are continuously changing water characteristics which have made water purification a difficult task. The water can no longer be treated easily with simple methods; bacteria, viruses, contaminants, waste products, heavy metals are finding their way into water.

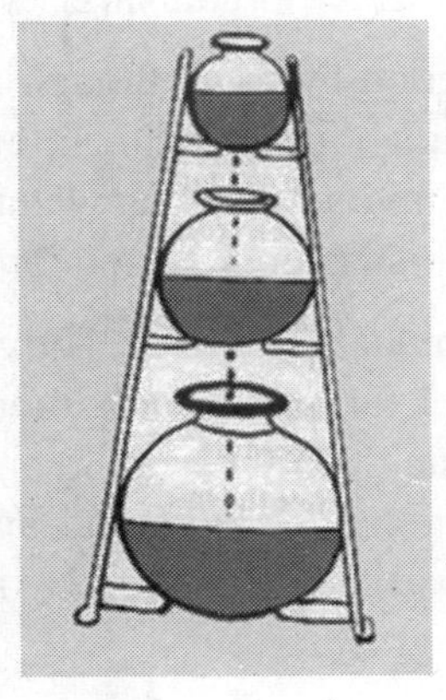

MICRONS	.0005	.001	.005	.01	.05	.1	.5	1	5	10	50	100

Polio Virus
Range of Electron Microscope
Carbon Block
Smallest Bacteria
Tobacco Smoke
Smallest Yeast
Range of Optical Microscope
Red Blood Cell
Smallest Particle Visible to Naked Eye
Human Hair

Reverse Osmosis
Conventional Filtration
Ultrafiltration
Microfiltration
Ionic Range
Macromolecular Range
Micron Particles
Fine Particles

Take a look at the contaminants that harbour water, and their comparative sizes: you will understand how difficult it would be to remove them and make water safe.

Everything that goes down our drains, on our lawns, on our agricultural fields or into the environment by any means eventually returns with a slap into water we drink. Unlike in the past, water purification now requires a technological expertise. There have been numerous methods to purify water from the good old three pot method to the present day RO systems. None is perfect. Often the best solution is a combination of methods. If you don't have a purification system, boiling, disinfecting and distillation are the methods that will kill most microbes in water.

Boiling is the safest method of purifying water which can destroy bacteria & viruses but it fails to remove dissolved impurities like pesticides, rust and harmful salts. Boil water for 3-5 minutes, cool it and drink it. But the taste would be bland, because the oxygen also boils out. Pour the water back and forth between two clean containers, oxygen would be back in and water will taste better.

Bleaching is an age old method; municipalities do this at their reservoirs, of course. Use only regular household liquid bleach that contains 5.25 percent sodium hypochlorite (household bleach) which disinfects and kills microorganisms.

Distillation is another good method, though a little difficult at home. It actually removes some microbes that pass through boiling and disinfecting and also removes heavy metals, salts and many chemicals. The process involves boiling water and then collecting the vapours. Vapours condense back to water and now this water does not contain salt and other impurities.

Candle filters were fashionable until recently though they are still being used. Water is filtered down to a bottom vessel through one or more ceramic filters which contain micro-pores. They block anything larger than the pore size. So only bacteria, protozoa, and microbial cysts which are larger than the pores are removed but others and viruses may pass through the filter. They can only remove the suspended particles but cannot kill bacteria. The bacteria entering the filter may pass through or stays put and grow within.

But filters are still used in the front end of almost all water purifiers. Spun polypropylene, porous plastic, ceramics, kdf, membranes, iodinated resin, ion exchange resins are some of the materials used as the filters to reduce sediment, dirt and turbidity.

In the present day conditions of water borne impurities, the line of attack should be multi-pronged, apart from the straight filtering through micro-porous filters. Granulated activated carbon, UV filtration, reverse osmosis are some of the methods. Let us look at the more sophisticated systems presently in use domestic water purification.

GAC and UV Water Filters: The candle filters can only block the physical contaminants, the bacteria and viruses may pass through these filters, even harbour colonies inside. In the present conditions of prevalent water borne diseases, it is essential to adopt better systems.

Granular Activated Carbon (GAC) is one of the most powerful sources to reduce traces of chlorine, industrial chemicals and a host of organic contaminants. Carbon removes contaminants through adsorption, as one pound of activated carbon has the equivalent surface area of a 160 acre farm. Then it acts as a catalyst to change the chemical composition of some contaminants. Water flowing through a GAC filter actually tastes better. However bacteria can survive within a carbon filter. So, the next line of attack would be purification by ultraviolet rays[10].

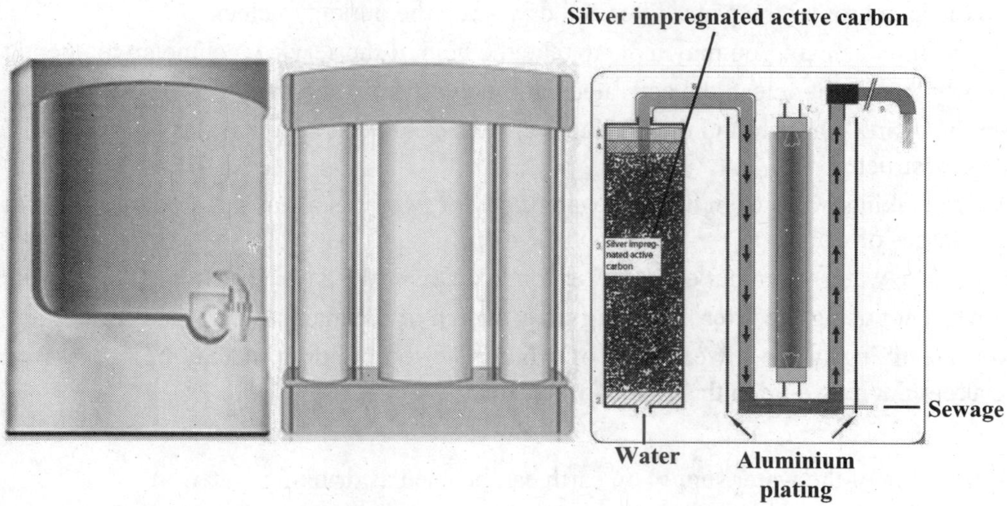

Ultraviolet rays attack the genetic core of the microorganisms and hence the microorganism's ability to function and reproduce is destroyed. The process destroys 99.99 percent of harmful microorganisms without adding chemicals to the water. It is easy and efficient. UV lamp is enclosed within a clear quartz sleeve and the water flows outside the quartz tube. UV does not change the taste, odour or colour of the water, but kills microorganisms. They cannot remove dissolved impurities like: rust or harmful chemicals like pesticides, arsenic, fluoride, heavy metals, etc. So, it is always necessary to install a sediment pre-filter and activated carbon post-filter along with the UV filtration.

In a typical UV filtration system, the water is first filtered through the sediment filter made up of multi-layered spun polypropylene. Physical impurities present in the water such as dust, dirt and mud are removed here. Then the next filter with activated carbon reduces color, odour, organic, chemical impurities and chlorine. The carbon is impregnated with silver to stop the growth of bacteria within the filter (bacteriostatic). Then the water flows through a UV chamber. Some manufacturers call this *e-boiling*; it eliminates bacteria, virus and protozoa. The UV chamber with

10 Ultraviolet or 'UV' is a type of energy found in the electromagnetic spectrum, lying between X-rays and visible light. Sunlight has long since been known to kill microorganisms. The rays from the sun contain the UV spectrum although at much lower intensities. Ultraviolet systems use special lamps that emit UV light of a particular wavelength, 254 nanometers (nm)

its UV light and quartz tube is housed in anodized aluminium chamber to increase the reflectivity of UV rays. After a few seconds of stabilization the water flows out of outlet tap.

There are a few facilities in many systems like auto-shut off when there is no use of the system for about 10 minutes. Another feature watches the turbidity of water, there by the purity. An electronic sensor eye monitors the purity of water and shuts down the system if the purity is not 100%. The unit also automatically switches off the UV lamp if the purifier is not used for 10 minutes, enhancing the life of the UV lamp. There is also interlock which shuts down the system if the UV lamp is not lighted up or if there is too much scaling around quartz glass that surrounds the UV lamp.

Care and Tips

- ✓ Keep the area around the water filter and dry. Keep the outlet tap clean.
- ✓ Keep the filters clean. You may have to take the help of the service technician to attend this.
- ✓ Similarly thoroughly clean the activated carbon every now and then.
- ✓ Keep the quartz glass around the UV lamp always clean. If it becomes dirty or opaque, UV rays will be obstructed.
- ✓ If you are taking water from it after a gap of day or two, it is always a good idea to throw away three glasses of water.
- ✓ Do not store water taken out of UV filter for more than two days. Use fresh filtered water.
- ✓ If you are not using the filter for a long time, switch of the mains supply and water inlet.
- ✓ If you are living in the lower floors of a multi-storied building, it may be necessary to fix a pressure reducing valve in the inlet of water line.

- Less than 1% of the water supply on earth can be used as drinking water.
- A person can live about a month without food, but only about a week without water. If a human does not absorb enough water dehydration is the result.
- Most of the earth's surface water is permanently frozen or salty.
- When water contains a lot of calcium and magnesium, it is called hard water.
- Bottled water can be up to 1000 times more expensive than tap water and it may not be as safe.
- Did you know that 25% of the bottled water on the market is drawn from municipal taps?
- Pure water (solely hydrogen and oxygen atoms) has a neutral pH of 7, which is neither acidic nor basic.

Reverse Osmosis

The type of purification adopted depends on the quality of your water. Carbon and UV filters can adequately effectively handle quite a lot of impurities giving you pure and safe water. But it is becoming more and more complicated as the water is getting contaminated with physical, organic and microbiological impurities from hospital wastes to industrial wastes to reckless use of water. These result in various water-borne diseases. Add to this water from multitude of bore wells, hard and brackish water which contain high levels of TDS (Total dissolved solids more than 500 mg/litre). So, our next level attack would be reverse osmosis water purifier.

In a Reverse osmosis systems[11], untreated water or tap water is forced through a semi-permeable membrane, in effect, water passes from a more concentrated solution to a more dilute solution through a semi-permeable membrane. This special membrane allows only the water to pass through, while impurities and contaminates are returned to the drain separately, rather than block them. The membrane's pores are so fine that it can remove contaminants and particles larger than .001 microns. Bacteria or cyst are passed out separately through the drain. Drinking water is purified without our own addition of chemicals like chlorine, bromine or iodine but with addition of good taste, odor and appearance.

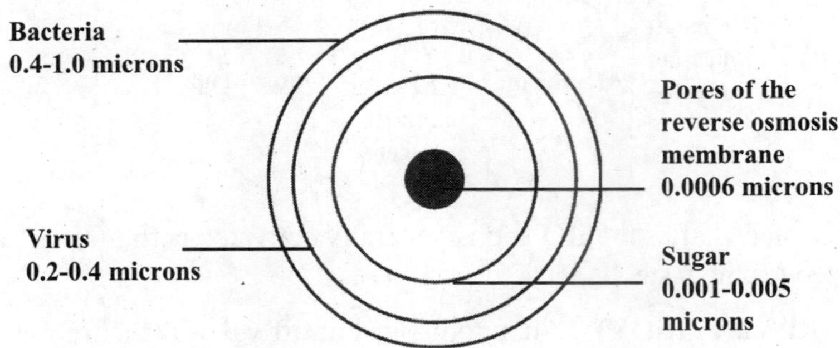

A standard RO system additionally consists of both pre- and post-filters which add to the additional contaminant removal and protect the membrane.

How It Works?: RO is the process by which water molecules are forced through a 0.0001 micron semi-permeable membrane by water pressure. Long sheets of the membrane are ingeniously sandwiched

11 High-pressure reverse osmosis systems have been used for years to desalinate water – to convert brackish or seawater to drinking water.

together and rolled up around a hollow central tube in a spiral fashion, called as a spiral wound membrane. Typically, a membrane for home water treatment is about 2" in diameter and 10" long.

It is housed in a container so water under pressure can be maintained on its surface. Water under pressure is forced through the membrane, separating it from unwanted substances. Interestingly, the rejects do not stay put and build up in RO systems as in the conventional systems. All those contaminants are diverted to the drain with the help of untreated water. That also gives longer life to the RO membranes.

Basic components common to all reverse osmosis systems:

Inlet Water Valve: Water to the RO filter is supplied through this valve. Normally, a tube connects RO with this.

Pre-filter (s): From there water enters into pre-filters, one or more often made of spun polypropylene. They remove sediments like dirt, salts and other foreign matter. Sometimes, carbon filters are also used to remove chlorine, which can spoil membranes.

Reverse Osmosis Membrane[12] : It is the heart of the system. They are spiral wound as shown in the picture here. Common materials are CTA (cellulose tri-acetate) and TFC/TFM (Thin film composite/material). Chlorine in water can spoil the later membrane.

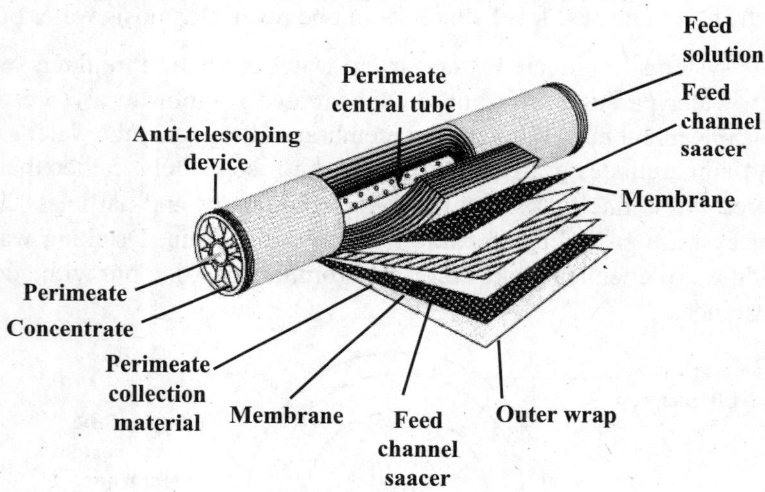

Post-filter(s): It is placed after the RO and is generally activated carbon. It actually removes any bad odors and improves the taste.

Automatic Shut Off Valve (SOV): An automatic shut off valve is incorporated in storage type RO systems. It prevents water from overflowing.

Check Valve: Similarly a non-return valve is placed at the outlet end of the RO membrane housing to prevent backward flow to the membrane. A backward flow can rupture the RO membrane.

12 The process of osmosis through semi-permeable membranes was first observed in 1748 by Jean-Antoine Nollet, a French clergyman and physicist. For the next 200 years, osmosis was only a laboratory curiosity. Then Loeb and Srinivasa Sourirajan discovered the techniques for making asymmetric membranes in 1959-60, which revolutionized desalination and water purification methods. Interestingly, it is a natural process in Seagulls. They have a semi-permeable membrane in the back of their neck which allows it to drink sea water sans all salt and contaminants.

Flow Control: The flow control is located in the RO drain line or waste water line tubing. Without flow control on the drain line, all the incoming water would simply flow down the drain line taking the path of least resistance. Flow control valve regulates water flow through the RO membrane.

Faucet: It is the point from where you can take water for drinking.

Drain Line: This line takes the waste water with all its impurities and contaminants to the drain from the outlet end of the reverse osmosis membrane housing. The flow control is also installed in this line.

Pump: In most systems, there is a small little pump to pump water at a high pressure so that water could be filtered through the semi-permeable membrane.

Care and Tips

✓ The heart and soul of any reverse osmosis water purification system is the membrane. So, please take care of it. Not all membranes are the same and plenty of cheap ones are available in the market.

✓ Good Quality reverse osmosis water purifiers should have 4 separate multi-stage pre-filters and one post-filter. Never purchase a RO system that doesn't have at least 4 filter stages.

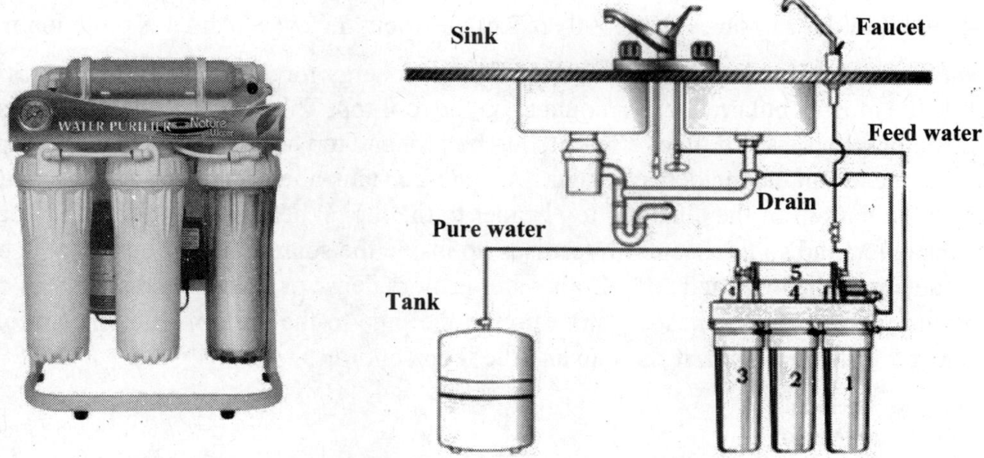

✓ RO systems work more efficiently when used frequently. Use RO water for everything, cooking, and coffee, everything apart from drinking.

✓ About once a month, completely drain the storage tank.

✓ Clean all the filters if the production rate is low. You may have to renew if they are very bad. If not solved, replace flow control and non-return valve. Finally the membrane.

✓ The carbon post-filter cartridge should be replaced if an unpleasant taste or smell occurs in the water.

✓ The R/O system is designed for the cold water supply only. Do not connect to hot water. RO membrane will soon get worse.

Solar Water Heaters

Those were the days when an Indian day used to start with a prayer to the Sun God, and the Surya Namaskar! Sun shone high but we started praying the mortal Gods. We are returning to the Sun again[13]. Yes, actually! Solar inverters are becoming popular. Increasingly solar powered water heaters are being used. Solar water heaters are cost-effective way to make hot water for your home, particularly in these power crisis-ridden days. The fuel is free- sunshine. By storing hot water in an insulated tank, hot water can be drawn any time, barring a few days, throughout the year. Solar collectors are installed typically on the roof tops. A 100 litre per day solar heater is suitable for 3-4 people and it can save up to 1500 units of electricity in a year. And it is pollution free.

There are several different ways to heat water by solar energy for domestic use. The thermo-syphon system is the most popular which is mounted on the roof top. This simple system consists of a solar heat collector with series of tubes connected to bottom and top headers. The collector is placed in a inclined plane to suit the incidence of sunrays. A storage tank above connects these headers, bottom header to the bottom of the tank and top header to the top. When water is heated, it becomes less dense or lighter, and so the heated water rises up inside the solar collector through the connecting pipe to the top of the insulated tank. Cold water is more dense or heavier and so it goes down from the bottom of the insulated header tank through the pipe to the bottom of the solar collector. As solar energy heats this water, it rises up and the loop continues.

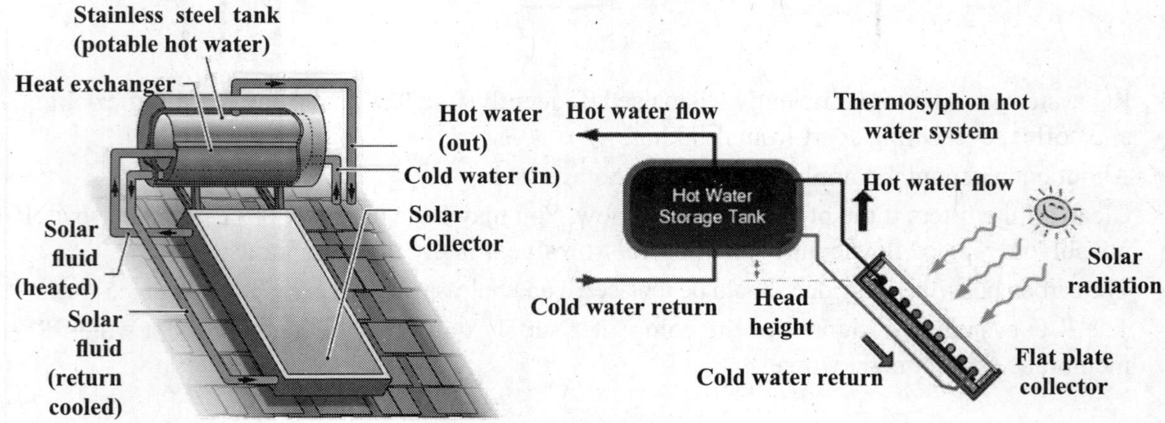

13 Earlier, solar water heaters were bare metal tanks painted black and tilted to face the sun to absorb heat. They could not store heat in the night. In 1909, William J. Bailey patented a solar water heater with a thin solar collector (black tank) and a separate insulated hot water storage tank.

However, for the thermo-syphon to work correctly, certain 'head height' must be maintained. So, the base of the water storage tank must be situated at least 1 to 2 feet (300 to 500 mm) above the top of the flat plate collectors. Total weight of water, storage tank, collector and piping must be considered when installing any solar heater on top of the roof.

This system is known as the direct circulation system. The water in this system can freeze in certain climates which are prone to freezing temperatures. So there are systems, where pumps circulate a non-freezing, heat-transfer fluid through the collectors and heat exchangers which indirectly heat the water.

Indirect Hot Water System: In this model, the solar collector contains antifreeze solution (typically a 50% Glycol/water mixture) which is circulated by a pump from the collector to a heat exchanger inside a storage tank. The heat exchanger is a copper coil inside the lower part of the storage tank or a flat plate exchanger. The heat exchanger transfers the solar heat from the collector's antifreeze solution to the water in the water storage tank.

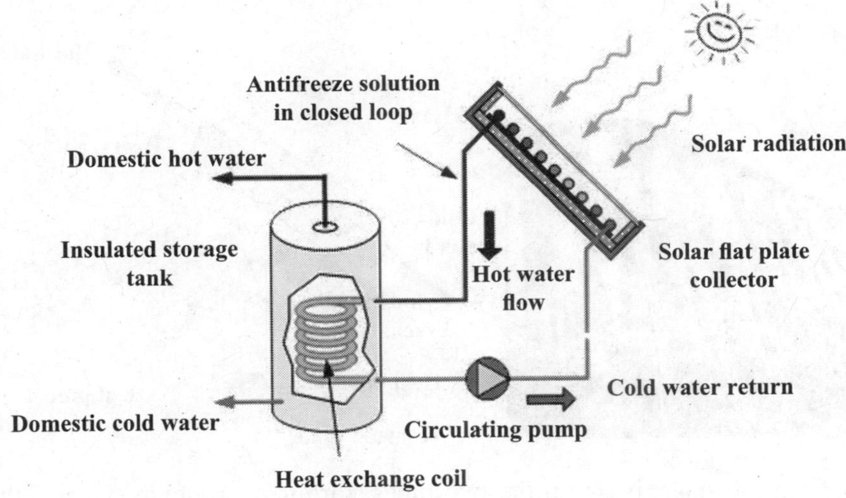

Solar Flat Plate Collectors: This is another design in the direct heat type known as a solar flat plate collector. It consists of a heat absorbing plate made up of a large copper or aluminium sheet.

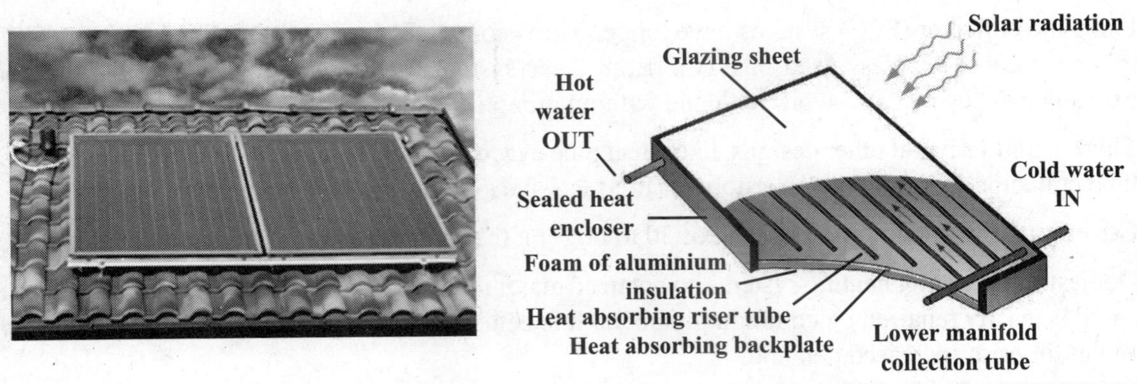

Both these metals are good conductors of heat and additionally to improve its efficiency the sheet is painted or chemically etched black to absorb as much solar radiation as possible. Several parallel copper pipes or tubes called risers are fixed on directly to the absorber plate to ensure maximum surface contact.

Sun heats the absorbing plate and in turn water in the tubes. Flat plate collectors are more cost-effective, simpler design, and installation is easier compared to other solar heaters. However, they are at their maximum efficiency when the sun is directly overhead at high noon. So to solve this problem and improve its efficiency further we have the evacuated tube collector.

Solar Evacuated Tube Collectors: Evacuated tube collectors perform well even during low sunlight times such as early in the morning or late in the afternoon, or during cloudy and cold conditions. They are made up of rows of parallel, transparent glass tubes supported on a frame. They are actually 'twin-glass tubes' with a thick glass outer tube and a thinner glass inner tube. The tubes are generally the strong, high temperature borosilicate glass with high transmittance for solar irradiation.

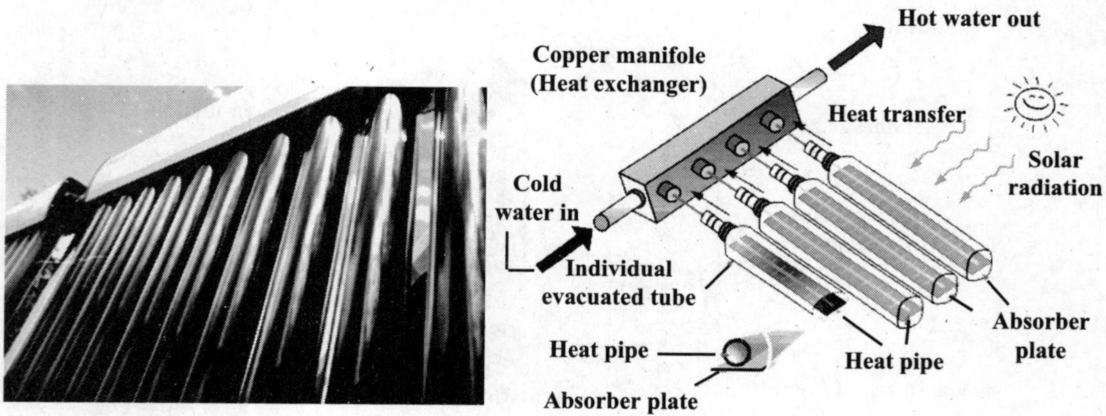

Air is evacuated from the space between the two tubes, forming a vacuum (Hence, they named evacuated tubes). This vacuum acts as an insulator reducing any heat loss. A copper tube with a fin attached to it runs through the inner tube. A number of these copper pipes are connected to a common header which is then connected to a storage tank. These solar heaters are more modern and more efficient and can reach high temperatures.

Flat plate collector (FPC) systems have longer life as compared to Evacuated tube collector (ETC) system because of glass used in ETCs. Both these systems are available with and without heat exchanger. They can also work with and without pump.

There are still several other designs, like, Heat pipe evacuated tube collectors, Direct flow evacuated tube collector, Integral collector storage (ICS) Passive system, Parabolic trough reflector.

Government subsidises to the extent of 30 to 60% on their purchase to different category of users.

Domestic solar water heating systems do not need major maintenance regularly. Occasional leakages could be easily repaired by common plumbers. It is better to keep a backup system for cloudy days and at times of increased demand.

Care and Tips: There are some tips for common problems of solar heaters.

- ✓ If there is no water in tap and no cold water supply, probably the valve is closed, line is plugged with foreign material or there is air lock in the pipes.
- ✓ If the cold water flow is normal, but water not heated at all, probably the collector is shaded or dusty, or it is plugged due to scaling. Also please check if you are consuming more than the generation of hot water.
- ✓ However, if water is not hot enough or quantity of hot water is not enough, the probable reasons are dirty collector, cloudy weather, high consumption, frequent opening and closing of hot water tap. There may be partial plugging of the collector. There may be vapour lock in the collector.
- ✓ If the hot water quantity is less, the reason again may be vapour lock or pinched or bent inlet/outlet pipes.
- ✓ To release vapour lock, allow the system to cool and drain it. Fill it again slowly.

Solar Cooker

Solar cooking is the simplest, safest, most convenient way to cook food without consuming fuels or heating up the kitchen. You can cook food, heat water, sanitize vessels.

There are numerous reasons to cook the natural way, with the Sun. Solar cookers are smoke-free and there are no fumes to burn your eyes or irritate your lungs. They do not cause accidental fires. As they are on the roof top, they are away from children. Solar cooking is slow but effective and it is difficult to burn food. Food can simply be left to cook in a solar cooker and you can use the free time for other chores. Solar cookers are portable which can be used anywhere you like, on camp sites, picnics or trekking. A cooker sufficient for a family of 4 to 5 can actually save about 3 or 4 LPG gas cylinders in a year. Average life is beyond 10 years.

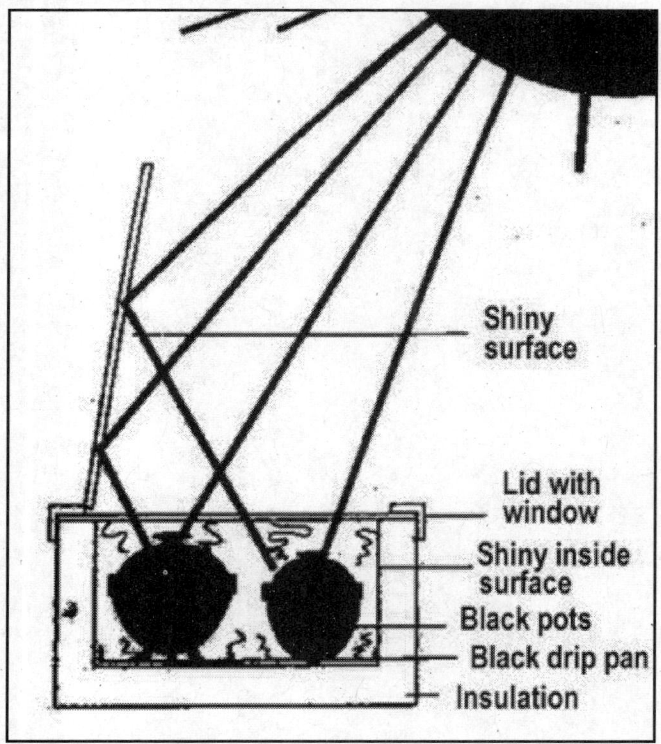

But solar cookers may not work properly in cloudy weather and near the poles, and in the evenings, when we would dine together with the family. Strong winds may also cool and disturb the process of cooking. For most effective cooking and for maximum efficiency, solar cooker needs to be placed directly towards the sun or in other words 'track' the sun. This does not mean that you sit in the Sun and continually adjust the cooker. The best time for solar cooking is at midday.

Fuel: Sunlight: Most solar cookers work on basic principles: sunlight is converted to heat energy which is retained for cooking. Abundantly available sunlight is the 'fuel,' but we need to concentrate, absorb and retain it.

Reflective mirror of glass, polished metal or metallic film is used to concentrate the light and heat from the sun onto the cooking area, effectively increasing its heating power.

Dark colors absorb the heat and the dark surfaces get very hot in sunlight. Absorption of the sun's energy is best when a surface is dark in color, thus the interiors are usually painted black. Dark, shallow, and thin metal pots are used with dark, tight-fitting lids.

The next important principle is the retention of that heat. Uncovered and improperly insulated solar cooker will quickly lose all its energy. A clear, heat-resistant plastic bag or large inverted glass bowl (in panel cookers) or an insulated box with a glass or plastic window (in box cookers) lets in sunlight, but keeps the heat in tact.

Designs: The three most common designs of solar cookers are – heat-trap boxes, curved concentrators (parabolics) and panel cookers.

Box Cookers: Most widely used solar cookers are box cookers. They are simple, easy to manufacture and use. They are made up of darkened sheet steel or aluminium and the box itself is well insulated to withstand temperatures up to 150°C (300°F). A transparent glass or plastic top covers the box. Linings of shiny foil or metal are provided on the inside to reflect and concentrate sunlight into the box. Blackened vessels are recommended for cooking.

Curved Concentrator Cookers: Curved concentrator cookers, or 'parabolics,' cook faster and to high temperatures but require frequent adjustment and supervision for safe operation. They are especially useful for large-scale institutional cooking. Old abandoned satellite dish can be very effective cooker when lined with aluminum foil on the inside surface. For that matter, even an umbrella can be treated like this with a foil lining to make a useful solar cooker. But be careful, the focal point and cooking pot can be very hot and the glare from the focused solar energy can be very severe. Please wear apporpriate protection.

Panel Cookers: Panel cookers are combination of box and curved concentrator cookers. They are simple and relatively cheaper and often used in large scale cooking. Cooking pots are enclosed in a clear plastic bag.

Apart from these, there are other designs of solar cookers such as Parabolic reflectors, Paraboloidal reflectors, Parabolic troughs, Spherical reflectors, etc.

Solar Water Pasteurization: Solar cookers can be effectively used for pasteurization. Pasteurization is a process of exposing food to heat effectively killing many of the disease-causing organisms. Milk is pasteurized at around 70ºC (160ºF). Heating water to 65ºC (150ºF) for a short period of time kills microbes like *Escherichia coli*, Rotaviruses, Giardia and the Hepatitis A virus.

Tips For Most Effective Cooking[14]

✓ Frequently clean the cooker of dust, stains, spills etc. Not only reduce all these would its efficiency but also reduce its life.

14 There is an entire village that uses only solar cooking- Bysanivaripalle, a silk-producing village, 125 km northwest of famed temple town Tirupati in Andhra Pradesh.

- ✓ It is often necessary to open the lid for checking the food. So uncover it as little as possible to avoid losing heat as it takes longer to recoup the lost heat.
- ✓ With certain food preparations it helps to pre-boil the water beforehand and later add in the ingredients such as corn, potatoes etc.
- ✓ When you are not using it for cooking a meal, why not put it to a good use like boiling water or drying some food stuffs.

Electricity

We just cannot live without electric power and one of the most dreaded fears now is the power cut. We harness electricity to make our lives comfortable. Its effects are countless and uses innumerable. But what is electricity? Basically there are two types of electricity, the way it travels.

One is Direct Current (DC) which is a constant stream of charges in one direction. Batteries, fuel cells and solar cells all produce direct current (DC). Batteries have positive (+) and negative (-) terminals.

The power supply into our households is Alternating Current (AC) which is a stream of charges that reverses direction continuously. The direction of the current reverses, or alternates, 50 times per second in India. It's cheaper and easier to make devices for AC power because you can increase and decrease the current for AC power very easily. Also AC power comes in types; single phase, or three phases.

The three most basic units in electricity are – voltage (V) measured in volts, current (I) measured in amperes and resistance (R) measured in ohms.

Just take a water pipe to understand these terms. The voltage is equivalent to the water pressure, which depends on the level from which the water flows or the potential difference, the current is equivalent to the flow rate, and the resistance is like the pipe size. The voltage is coming out of a simple dry battery cell is 1.5 volts DC whereas that coming out of domestic wiring is 230 volts AC and is lethal.

Electrical power is measured in watts. In an electrical system power (P) is equal to the voltage multiplied by the current.

Let us see some of the effects of electricity which translate into our comfort.

1. Mechanical Effect: Look around your house and you will find that it is filled with electric motors. Electric motors are everywhere! No modern home should be without one or may be a dozen. You'll find a motor in the fan, fridge, washing machine, and the little pump that pumps water to the roof tank.

2. Chemical Effect: Best example for a chemical effect of electricity is Electroplating. It is electrochemical process of deposition of a thin metal layer onto another, say gold layer on copper. When you see a gold plated jewelry, think of electricity.

3. Thermal Effect: Heating effect is used in the heaters, irons and geysers. An electric current passing through a conductor raises its temperature. Higher the resistance of the conductor, higher would be the heat. Copper offers least resistance, so we use it in the household wiring. Nichrome offers higher resistance which is used as a heating element.

4. Magnetic Effects: Motors to loud speakers, magnetic effect is what works for us most. Electricity passing through a wire causes magnetism around it which is called an electromagnetism. Interestingly if a wire in a magnetic field moves, current is produced in the wire so also in the wire

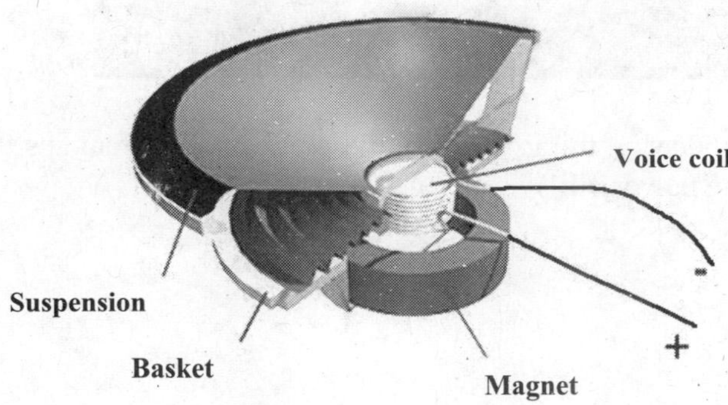

within a moving magnetic field. That's the principle by which motors and generators work. Thanks to Michael Faraday!

5. Physiological Effect: That's the shock you get when you touch live wire, which is dangerous. Controlled shock treatment is used to treat mental disorders. The body gives out typical signals by which the sensors can take readings about your heart or brain. Heart pacemakers use effectively to keep the heart beating in certain cases.

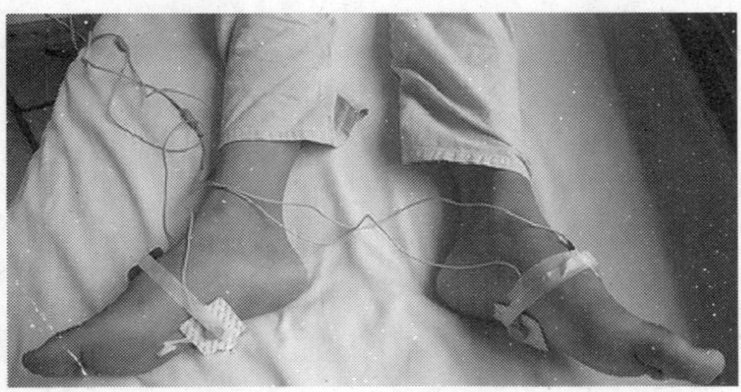

6. Photoelectric Effect: Electricity under certain conditions can produce photoelectric effect. This of course is seen in our televisions, cameras and numerous automatic applications. Good old tungsten bulbs light up because of heat but present CFL bulbs and LEDS are the result of photoelectric effect.

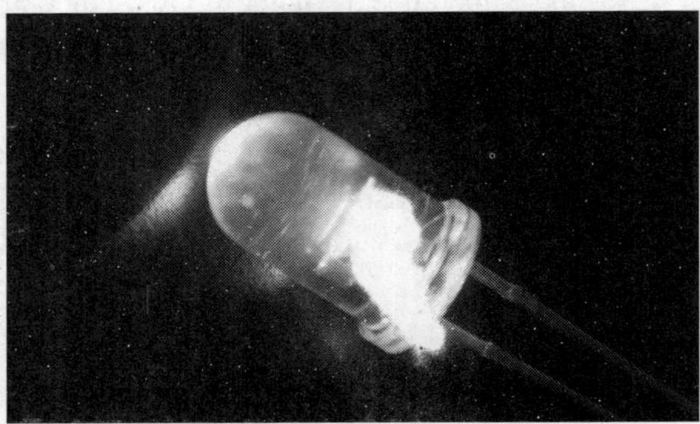

We now learn about the wonderful things that use these effects to provide us the pleasure, (Well! A little pain when you pay the power bill!)

Battery Cells

Nowadays our lives revolve around battery cells. We use them in our torch lights, transistor radios, remote controls. We have them in our cars. They give us power back up in the invertors when the power fails. I feel amused when people grope in the moving train from compartment to compartment to find a plug socket for their cell phones. How our lives are compartmentalized by these battery cells! It will be useful to know a bit of batteries.

Presently we have a variety of cells or batteries to choose from; lead acid, zinc carbon, nickel cadmium and Nickel metal halide, lithium, silver oxide and what not[15]! Cell is a storage form of electrical energy. It produces electric current without the use of moving parts, like those in generators.When two or more cells are used, it is known as battery, but these words are used interchangeably often even to a single cell. These cells are fixed in series to get higher voltage and are kept in parallel to get higher current capacity. Their current capacity is measured in ampere hours(Ah). 1 Ah battery can discharge at a rate of one ampere for one hour, before it becomes dead and a 150 Ah can discharge 150 amperes in one hour. Smaller cells are rated in milliampere-hour (mAh). Batteries produce direct current (DC).

They transform chemical energy into electrical energy. Without going into technical jargon, we have cells that cannot be charged and those that can be charged. A primary cell cannot be recharged. Secondary cells can be charged as the chemical reactions inside can be reversed by applying proper electric current. They are also used as storage batteries. Each these cells have their own characteristics, like cell voltage, current capability, storage capacity and rechargeability. There are of many types and varieties of cells in use today and developments are continuously made[16].

Zinc-carbon Cells: Good old zinc carbon cells are the most common type. They show 1.5 volts between positive and negative terminals. They are available in various sizes known variously as AAA, AA,

---

15 Interestingly there are other cells, like solar cells. Also called photovoltaic cells, they convert the energy of visible light into electricity. Those produce electricity from heat energy are known as thermoelectric cells. Nuclear batteries convert the radiation emitted by radioactive substances into electricity. A fuel cell converts the chemical energy of a fuel say from hydrogen and oxygen directly into electrical energy.

16 Count Alessandro Volta, an Italian scientist made the first battery around 1800. The potential difference, measured in Volts, one of primary electrical characteristics is named after him.
Gaston Plant built the first storage battery in 1859, with lead plates immersed in sulfuric acid, a system same as the present day lead-acid batteries
Georges Leclanche, a French chemist developed the carbon-zinc in the late 1860's.

BB, CC etc. This nomenclature denotes the capacity and dimensions of each cell but all these cells show a voltage of 1.5 volts. The voltage drops as the cell is used. These are not normally rechargeable.

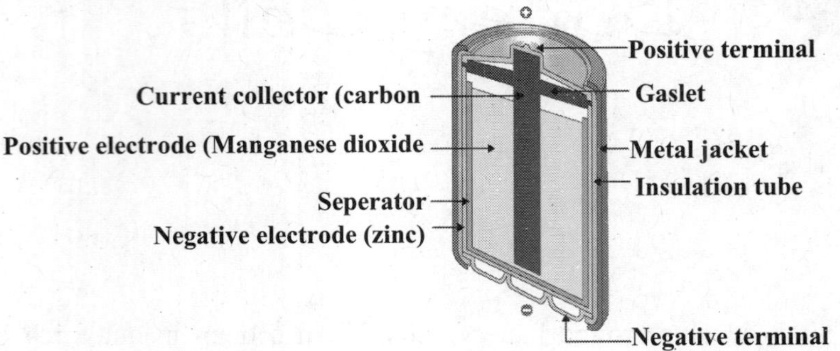

In the typical zinc-carbon cell, a zinc can serves as the negative electrode. The can is filled with a mixture of manganese dioxide, ammonium chloride, zinc chloride, and water which serves as the positive electrode after due separation from the can. A carbon rod is placed in this center which becomes the positive terminal. There is variation of these cells in alkaline cell or Alkaline Manganese cell. Unlike the zinc-carbon, this cell uses an alkaline electrolyte—potassium hydroxide. They last longer.

Nickel-cadmium Cells: Nickel cadmium cells show a voltage of 1.2 volts, which means that two cells in series show a voltage of 2.4 volts. Nickel-cadmium cells are available in the same sizes and shapes as zinc-carbon cells. Nickel hydroxide acts as a positive electrode and the negative electrode is composed of cadmium with an electrolyte of potassium hydroxide. These are rechargeable.

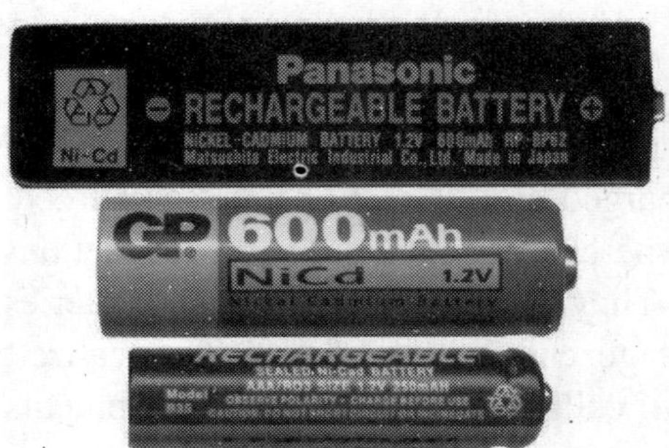

They suffer from a memory effect. If they are recharged after only partially discharged, they tend to recharge only to that partial extent rather than their full capacity. Nickel metal halide cells are also show a voltage of 1.2 volts and are rechargeable. They show certain better characteristics than nickel cadmium cells. They are environmentally friendly and do not show the memory effect of Ni-Cad cells.

Lead Acid Cells: Lead acid cells are most widely used for high power applications such as in automobiles, UPS systems, emergency lighting systems where weight of the battery has no concern but the capacity required is high. Lead acid batteries can deliver high currents and recharge cycles are high.

Generally lead-acid cell consists of positive and negative plates immersed in a solution of sulfuric acid and water. Perforated separators insulate the plates from each other. The negative plates are made up of porous lead. The positive plates are a lead grid filled with lead dioxide. Each cell voltage is 2 volts and in a typical car battery, six of such cells are connected in series in a single container to give 12 V. Battery condition of the lead-acid batteries is checked with a hydrometer

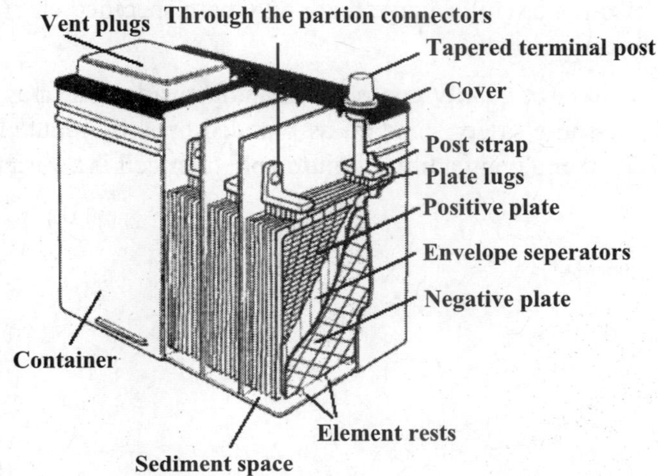

and a voltmeter. The specific gravity of the sulfuric acid in a cell is measured by the hydrometer, which indicates its state of charge. Voltage of the cell is measured by a voltmeter. Over period of use these batteries lose water in the electrolytic solution through evaporation or decomposition which has to be topped up.

Sealed lead acid batteries or maintenance free batteries are another form of the same where the electrolyte is within the moistened separators. Otherwise known as Calcium-lead batteries they do not require additional water. These batteries but are permanently sealed.

Silver Oxide Cell: Silver Oxide cell, also known as button cell is mostly commonly used in watches. The positive electrode is composed of silver oxide, zinc as the negative electrode (anode) and the electrolyte is sodium hydroxide (NaOH) or potassium hydroxide (KOH). They have greater energy densities than any conventional battery, next only to lithium cells.

Lithium Cells: Lithium ion cells power most of the portable equipment like cell phones, laptops; handy-cams. These have higher energy density. They have a cell voltage of 3.6 volts. In all lithium

cells the negative electrode is composed of lithium, but the positive electrode varies with different types, most common being manganese dioxide.

But the point of concern is that they have a flammable electrolyte kept in pressure. They should be always used with protection circuit. Charge them only with specified charger. Faulty chargers can upset the battery's protection circuit.

They are also built with strict quality control in manufacturing. Cheaper battery packs may not be manufactured to the same safety standard as branded ones by reputed manufacturers. Short-circuiting is risky and can end up in a fire. Lithium –polymer cell is a variation of those cells.

Motors

There's something magical about magnetism. As children, we marvelled at the magnets attracting metals like iron, nickel and cobalt but were non-plussed when the poles repulsed.

In 1831, Michael Faraday[17] formulated Faraday's laws of electromagnetic induction. That's the basis of almost all the electric marvels and the motors that move the modern amenities. Every electric current has a magnetic field surrounding it. In simple language, if a wire is placed in a magnetic field, electric current is induced if either the magnetic field is changing or the conductor is moving. Alternating currents have fluctuating magnetic fields. Electromagnetic induction occurs when a circuit with an alternating current flowing through it generates current in another circuit simply by being placed nearby.

In your house, almost every mechanical movement is caused by an AC (Alternating current) or DC (Direct current) electric motor. Let us see some motors.

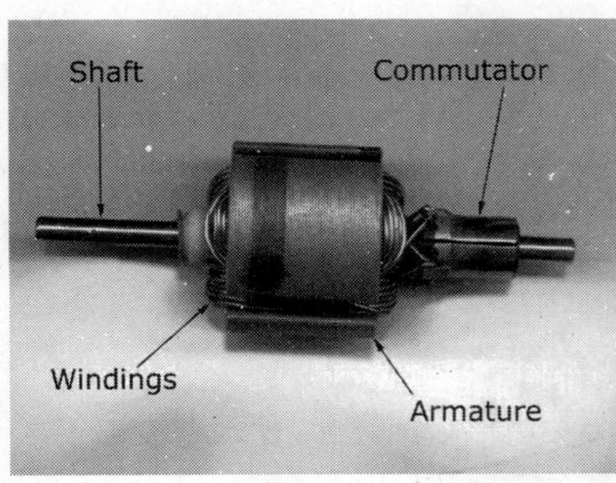

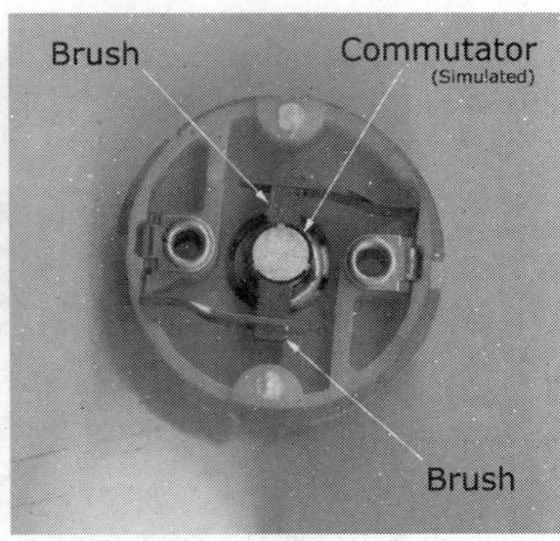

Almost all the toys, tape recorders, CD players work with DC motors. In a typical DC motor, there are permanent magnets on the outside and a spinning armature on the inside. The permanent magnets are stationary, so they are called the stator. The armature rotates, so it is called the rotor.

17 One of the first electromagnetic rotary motors was invented by Michael Faraday in 1821, and consisted of a free-hanging wire dipping into a pool of mercury. A permanent magnet was placed in the middle of the pool. When a current was passed through the wire, the wire rotated around the magnet, showing that the current gave rise to a circular magnetic field around the wire.

The armature contains an electromagnet with coils of insulated copper wire. When you turn electricity on these coils become electromagnets, create a magnetic field in the armature that attracts and repels the magnets in the stator. So, the armature spins through 180 degrees. To keep it spinning, you have to change the poles of the electromagnet. The brushes handle this change in polarity. Actually the DC is connected to the brushes. They make contact with two spinning electrodes attached to the armature and flip the magnetic polarity of the electromagnet as it spins.

AC Motors: AC motors generally come in two types: single phase and three phase.

Single-Phase AC Motors: The most common single-phase motor is the shaded-pole synchronous motor, which is most commonly used in devices requiring lower torque such as electric fans, microwave ovens and other small household appliances. Another common single-phase AC motor is the induction motor, commonly used in major appliances such as washing machines and clothes dryers.

Three-Phase AC Motors: Three phase motor is used for higher-power applications, but rarely in domestic applications. The rotor consists of a number of insulated copper conductors embedded in steel. Through electromagnetic induction, the rotating magnetic field induces current to flow in these conductors, which in turn sets up a counterbalancing magnetic field and this causes the motor to turn in the direction the field is rotating.

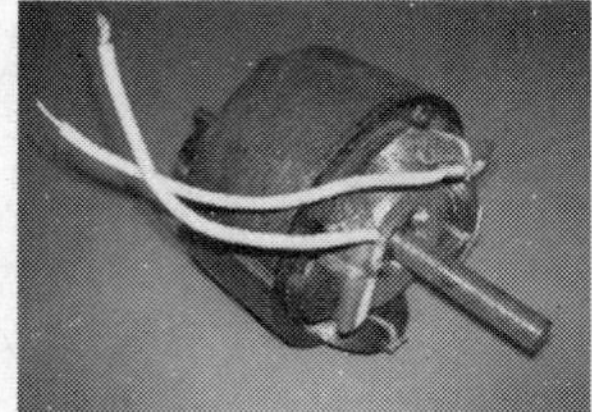

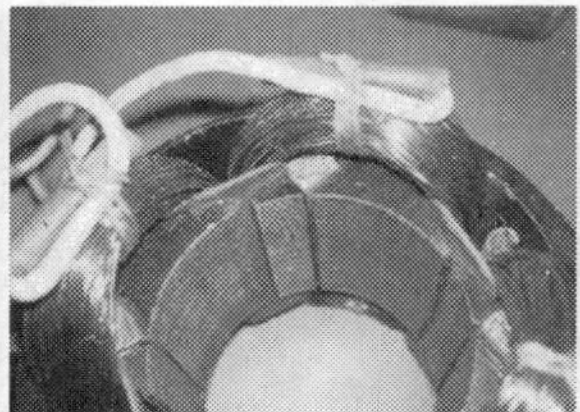

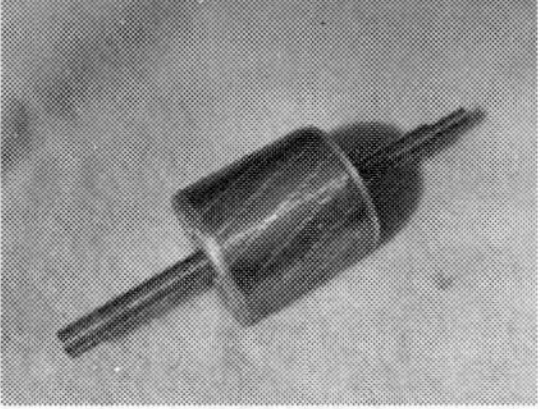

Universal Motors: Universal motors are used in most of the domestic appliances. These motors can work on both AC and DC. They can take high starting loads. They are compact in design

capable of high speeds. Different speeds are achieved by field coil windings with tapings connected through a switch.

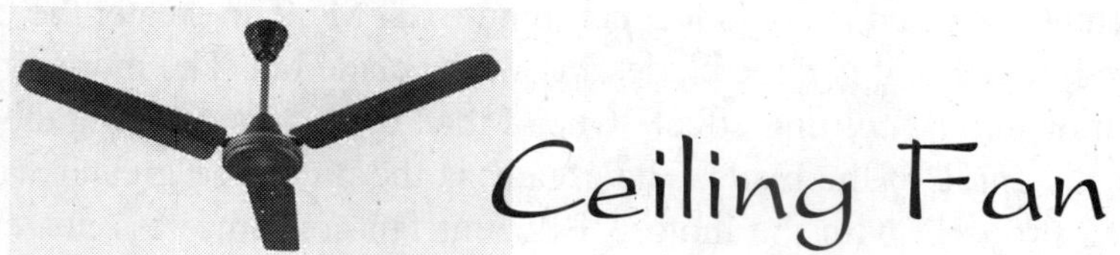

Ceiling Fan

When the electric power fails in a country like India, the first thing we would reach for is a good old hand fan. Seemingly simple device; three or four blades attached to a motor and the whole thing hung from the ceiling. When it stops, it makes our life miserable. Even the folks using air conditioner, keep a ceiling fan[18] in their rooms. Fans do not cool air, but they also do not guzzle power. Fans only slowly circulate air in an otherwise still, hot room. When the sweat evaporates, the body surface cools in a process known as evaporative cooling.

The key components of a ceiling fan are here:

Electric motor-Makes the fan blades move and circulate air. In India most of the ceiling fans are meant domestic power supply which is single phase 230 volts. Apart from the windings and electromagnetic core, these motors require a capacitor for starting, which is externally mounted on the fan.

Blades- Three or four blades usually made of metal, or plastic which are attached to the motor housing.

Hook- Secures the fan to the ceiling. Variations are 'J' hook, 'U' hook or 'S' hook

Rubber Bush- It is inserted between the hook and the bolt holding the fan. Reduces noise, absorbs starting and stopping shocks.

Down rod, a metal pipe used to suspend the fan from the ceiling. Length can be varied to suit the room size and distribution of air.

Canopies - enclose the hooks, connectors and starting capacitor.

Speed regulator- Older speed regulators had resistance type speed regulator which regulate fan speeds in 5 or 6 steps, but most modern fans have electronic regulators, either in step less or stepped forms. They save power in lower speeds.

While all ceiling fans may look same, they are not. First – fans come in sizes of 24", 36", 48", 56" with the end to end diameter of blades. The size of the room decides the size of the fan. If the room has high ceiling, you may need longer down rod. There should be at least 2.3 m or 7ft 6" from the floor to the bottom of the fan for safety. On average, a ceiling fan on full speed will consume about 75 watts.

18 The electric ceiling fan was invented in 1882 by Philip Diehl. Soon he had to face stiff competition from copycats. Earlier ceiling fans were driven by water turbines, using a stream of running water and system of belts. Philip Diehl introduced a lighting fixture to his fan making a two-in-one.

Air movement of a fan is measured in cubic feet per minute (CFM). The greater the CFM, the more air would be circulated, whether it is three blade fan or four blade fan. The more air is moved, the greater is the evaporation and its chilling effect. One of the key factors deciding the air movement is the blade pitch, or the angle of the blade. The greater is the pitch, the greater would be the air movement if designed properly with the motor. Efficient fan consume less power but circulate more CFM.

Care and Tips

- ✓ Mostly bad or cheaper bearings, imbalanced fan blades cause noise. Never interchange fan blades with other fan blades, even though it is similar or same model.
- ✓ Regularly check to ensure that all screws are tight. Over time, they may get loosened up. Then the fan may wobble or become noisy and is also unsafe. Fix all the washers, spring washers, screws for any given fan.
- ✓ It is a good idea to lubricate the fan once a year or two. However, modern fans have sealed bearings which are permanently lubricated.
- ✓ While sucking air and circulating it, fan also sucks dust which normally settles on the blades and also on the motor. Clean as often as necessary. Dusty fan blades can be noisy, can wobble and ultimately throw the dust on to you.
- ✓ Wobbling is caused by the weight of fan blades being out of balance with each other. This can happen if the fan blades are warped, not screwed tight, or blades of different weights, shapes or sizes are used as even minute differences do matter. Dust also does imbalance the fan blades.
- ✓ Electronic speed regulators may create hum on the fan in lower speeds.

Typical Ceiling Fan Components Illustrated

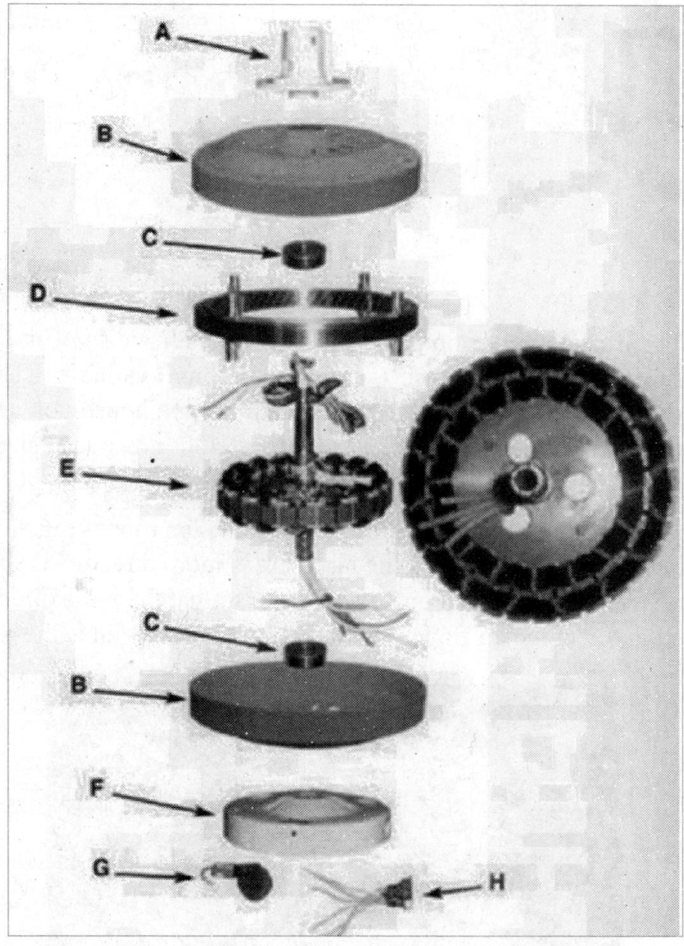

A Yoke – Accepts down rod.

B Motor Cover – Covers motor and centers rotor and stator.

C Bearing – Factory sealed insures smooth operation.

D Rotor – Transfers the magnetic energy from the stator.

E Stator

F Switch Housing

G Speed Switch

H Reverse Speed

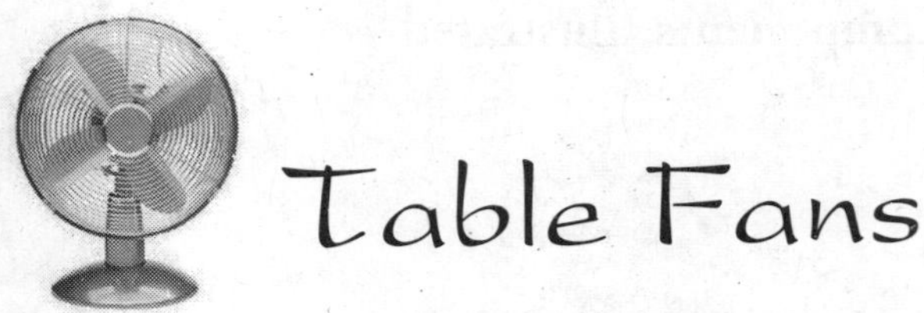

Table Fans

Table fans are also very popular in Indian homes because of their portability and also they can be used where there is no good ceiling available. They come handy when there are no ceiling hooks to mount a ceiling fan and in a rented house you are not allowed to fix a hook. Table Fans are manufactured 200 mm, 300 mm and 400 mm sweep sizes, but the one, which is most commonly used, is of 400 mm sweep size.

A table fan is little more complicated than ceiling fan. A table fan rotates much faster than ceiling fan. Compared to a ceiling fan, the breeze from the table fan is more directional. These fans also can be made to oscillate, meaning that it turns from side to side, so that the air is directed to all sides. These fans also can be tilted to direct the air flow. A variation of the table fan is the pedestal fan.

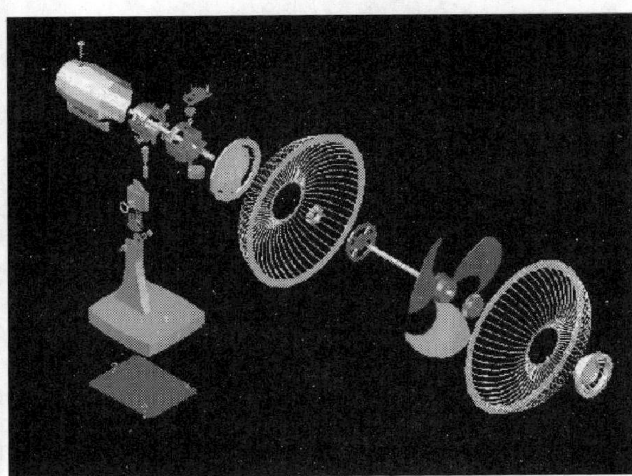

Table fans have sturdy, heavy base where the regulator, capacitor, etc are housed. The fan itself is fixed to a motor on a pivoted base, so that the fan head can be tilted. Fortunately the table fan blades come in single assembly which is screwed tight to the motor shaft. It is guarded on both sides with grills for safety.

The head contains all of the working parts of the fan. And there is a little gearbox attached also to the motor on the rear side. This gearbox makes the fan to oscillate. Actually, the fan head is on a dual pivot as the other pivot holds a lever to turn the entire fan head.

A knob on the fan head on the other end of the fan facilitates the oscillation on and off. A worm gear is attached to the motor. A worm shaft mates with the gear, when the knob is pushed down.

The other end of it is a lever is attached to the pivoted fan head. Thus, the rotation movement of the gear is turned into the side-to-side sweeping motion that makes the oscillating fan.

Typically, pushing the knob down activates the oscillation. When this knob is pressed down, the fan head starts turning in one direction. At the end of the stroke, it starts returning. The sequence continues. When the knob is pulled upward, the oscillation is off. You will notice that the knob slowly rotates when it is pressed down.

Care and Tips

✓ Most of the table fans are equipped with bush bearings. They need to be lubricated. Put a drop of sewing machine oil into the oil holes on the motor and watch how smoothly the fan rotates.

✓ It is a good idea to lubricate the fan once a year or two. A drop of oil on the gears, pivot pin and pivot bearings would help.

✓ Though the fan blades come as a single unit. Never interchange fan blades with other fan blades.

✓ The fan assembly is mounted on the motor shaft with a screw. It is screwed into a recess on the motor shaft. If it is loose the fan wobbles and slips. Ensure that all screws are tight.

✓ While sucking air and circulating it, fan also sucks dust which normally settles on the blades and also on the motor. Clean as often as necessary. Dusty fan blades can be noisy, can wobble and ultimately throw the dust on to you.

✓ Wobbling is caused by the weight of fan blades being out of balance with each other. If the fan blades are warped, bent or cracked, they become out of balance. Even minute differences do matter. Dust also does imbalance the fan blades.

✓ Electronic speed regulators may create hum on the fan in lower speeds.

Mixers, Blenders, Grinders and Food Processors

These have become such an indispensable kitchen aids taking away the drudgery of kitchen for the housewife. While electricity has taken over the hand operated ones, still they are used in certain household and by certain specialist cooks.

A hand mixer consists of a handle with a hand-operated crank on the side, geared to two beaters. The handle is held with one hand and the crank is turned with the other, turning the beaters which act on the food ingredients. Various attachments – each shaped differently are provided with a hand mixer to perform the mixing, folding, beating and whipping operations specifically.

An immersion blender, or 'stick blender' is still used to clarify butter from the curd and to convert it as butter milk. Present day mixer grinders offer multi-speciality devices with a number of blades to work with. They have virtually replaced the handheld mixers and grinders.

The mixing/grinding jar is a separate container which is fixed on top of a vertical motor and locked by a twist. A coupling connects the drive. Often two or three jars are supplied one small for *chutneys*, one large one made of glass with markings generally for fruit juices, and one stainless steel bowl for all other uses. This container is generally shaped in a way that the material to circulates through the blades, rather than simply spinning around.

There is a lid on the top and the blade assembly is in the bottom. It is this blade assembly makes all that of a mixer, grinder, or blender. Blenders are very different from mixers. Blenders are used more to chop, or break larger food items. They have sharp blades and operate at higher speeds compared to mixers. The blade assembly has a simple sealing mechanism which prevents the food ingredients from leaking down. Similarly, there is a gasket under the bowl where it mates the motor. Motors are multi-speed operated with a switch.

Food Processors[19] : Food processors are similar to blenders in many ways. Food processors have a number of interchangeable blades and attachments instead of two or three, designed for specific applications. Food processors can slice/chop, shred/grate vegetables, grind hard nuts, coconut kernel, seeds. They can puree, mix and knead dough. They are two drives connected to a single motor; one high speed and one low speed. They are interlocked so that only one can be used at a time. Main drive is mixer grinder while the side drive is a food processor. Wider and shorter

19 French catering company salesman, Pierre Verdun, produced a bowl with a revolving blade in the base to process food. Roger Perrinjaquet from Switzerland patented the immersion blender on March 6, 1950. The Polish-American Stephen J. Poplawski, owner of the Stevens Electric Company, patented the drink mixer in 1922. He also introduced the liquefier blender in 1922.

bowls are attached to the side drive which runs slow. A lid with a 'feed tube' is then fitted onto the bowl. A feed tube allows ingredients, vegetables or fruits to be inserted while the machine is chopping, grinding or pureeing.

Modern food processors have safety devices which prevent the motor from starting if the bowl is not properly fixed to the base or if the lid is not properly fixed to the bowl. Most of the present day, machines have a trip switch which stops the machine under overload. It has to be reset after a few minutes to start again, of course after the overload is removed.

Important Parts

Coupling: Generally made of reinforced rubber or tough plastic, it connects the motor to the grinding bowl and transfers the rotation. A matching part is fixed to the motor. It is connected to the cutter shaft by left hand thread, which means that you have to turn in the opposite direction of normal threads. It is a good idea to keep a spare on hand.

Cutters: Normally, two or three types of cutters are supplied with a grinder to accomplish different mixing or grinding jobs. Food processors have more number of cutters and attachments. Cutters are sharp.

Motors: The heart of a food machine is its motor. Universal motors are used in the mixers, grinders, and food processors. Different speeds are achieved by field coil windings with tapings connected through a switch.

Care and Tips: The following points are useful while selecting and using this kitchen appliance.

Wattage: Power consumed by motor 600/750 watts is normal wattage range for mixers.

RPM: Revolutions or rounds per minute made by the cutters in the bowl. Modern machines have speeds of 12,000-18,000 RPM higher the wattage higher the RPM, higher the heat and noise also. Please note that this is a very high speed; where as a typical ceiling fan runs at about 300 RPM.

Rating: It is an important parameter, which tells you how long the machine can be used continuously. 30 minutes is normal but it depends and is stamped on the machine. Do not cross it, the machine may overheat and burn out.

Safety: It is your life! Proper earthing is a must for your machine and house wiring. The third and stouter pin on the plug is meant for safe route of any electrical leakage to the ground. The third and stouter hole in an electrical outlet is connected to the earthing. Modern electrical outlets are built with an interlock which connect the main power only when the earth pin is connected. Do not remove this pin or defeat it.

Most of the modern machines are built with a cut out or trip switch to prevent overload of the machine. Do not defeat it by shorting it or by using a switch different amps setting.

Standardization: Buy the machine for which spares are generally available or face a headache later.

Care and Tips

- ✓ Whether it is mixer, grinder, blender and food processor, cleaning is a must immediately after the job is over. Cleaning is easy, pour a little water, run the machine for a few seconds and pour out the water; it almost cleans itself. Forget this, the leftover food gets solidified, jams the machine, next time you try, it would not start again.
- ✓ If the machine stops while in operation, it is warning that the machine is overloaded. Unplug it. Reduce the quantity, wait for a few minutes, reset the switch and start again.
- ✓ Keep the hands and utensils out of container while mixing to reduce the risk of injury.
- ✓ Keep the children away. Blades are sharp.
- ✓ Never use these devices without their covers in place.
- ✓ Do not mix hot liquids.
- ✓ Switch off when not in use. Switch if you are going out. To disconnect, pull the plug, not the cord.

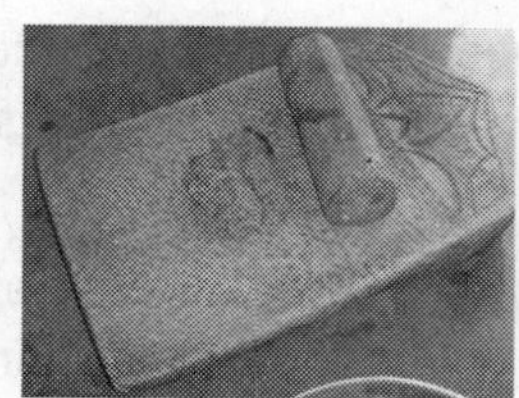

Wet Grinders

All those mixers, grinders, blenders and food processors are originally designed for the western cuisine. They are simply useless when it comes to making south Indian delicacies like idly, vada or dosa; add to it, kneading atta or wheat flour, or scrap coconuts. Because of the heat they generate, the batter would never be proper and the flavour and micronutrients would be lost. Alternative would be to go back to the good old, Mortar & Pestle (Kundi-Sotta) and Flat Stone (Sil-Batta). Enter the wet grinder.

In wet grinding, the grinding is accomplished by stone just as in the good old method, instead of high speed cutters and blades. Conventional electric wet grinder has one stone which can be removed and kept aside on its stand. After filling the ingredients, it can be replaced into the granite lined stainless steel drum. Entire drum rotates slowly due to gear mechanism driven by a motor. The revolving roller stones crush, mix, pound and grind simultaneously, so that all the ingredients are ground to exact proportions and are thoroughly mixed, retaining the nutrition value and also the desired taste. The grinder stones are made of hard, good quality granite, which would not chip

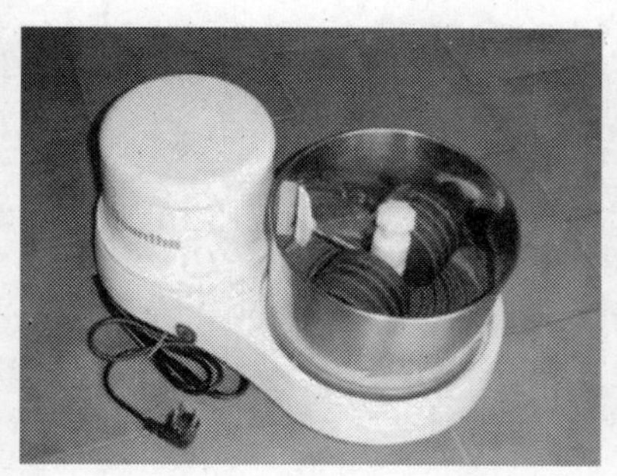

or powder during grinding applications, wet or dry. They can be removed for cleaning. The motor housing is usually made of ABS plastic. The plastic components used are made of food grade nylon. The power requirements are low for wet grinders in the order of 150 m watts because of low speed.

Variations of this are Table Top Wet Grinders and Tilting Type Wet Grinder. Basically both of them have the same features. Two roller stones are placed on the opposite sides in stainless steel drum with stone lining. They can be removed. In the tilting type wet grinder, the drum can be tilted to pour out the batter. No need to remove the stones or lift the drum. Stones can still be removed by opening a plastic nut.

Electric Roti Maker

When electricity passes through a wire, it heats because of the resistance offered by the wire. Gold, silver, copper and aluminium offer least resistance and they are very good conductors. So copper and aluminium are used in house wiring. Materials like wood, plastic are non-conductors as they do not conduct electricity at all. Tungsten, Nichrome are bad conductors as they offer very high resistance for electricity flow. When electricity is passed through these wires, they develop so much heat that they are used as a source for heating. As a matter of fact, tungsten becomes, red, later yellow, then white hot, an effect used in our electric bulbs. We make use of this heating effect in a number of our domestic needs such as room heaters, geysers, electric stoves, roti makers and irons.

It is of course a laborious process to make rotis in the traditional way, making dough, making round balls and rolling them. In fact, I could never learn the technique of rolling rotis, always ended up making India and Australia maps. Electric Roti maker reduces some of the steps in the roti making process. It cooks the roti without the need for rolling out the dough and replaces the rolling pin, rolling board, the frying pan (tawa) and the stove. Use of oil is reduced which contributes to better health. Gas is saved but electric power is spent.

A roti maker has two cooking plates made of die cast heavyweight aluminium or stainless steel on top and bottom to quickly and uniformly heat rotis without any hot spots or low spots. The plates are coated with non-stick material like Teflon for easy release and cleaning. Temperature is controlled automatically with a light signal showing when the temperature is reached.

But it takes a technique to make rotis in an electric roti maker. Preheat the maker before hand until the light goes of indicating sufficient heat. Take a ball of dough and make it a little flat, by pressing between both the palms. Place this flat ball near the lid of the maker, never in the centre.

Close the lid and keep heating. After two minutes you will find small bubbles on the roti. Then reverse it with a wooden or non-stick spatula. Close it again and hold it until roti to fluff up. Reverse it again.

- However rotis made in this maker become hard after a few hours. They have to be consumed while they are hot.

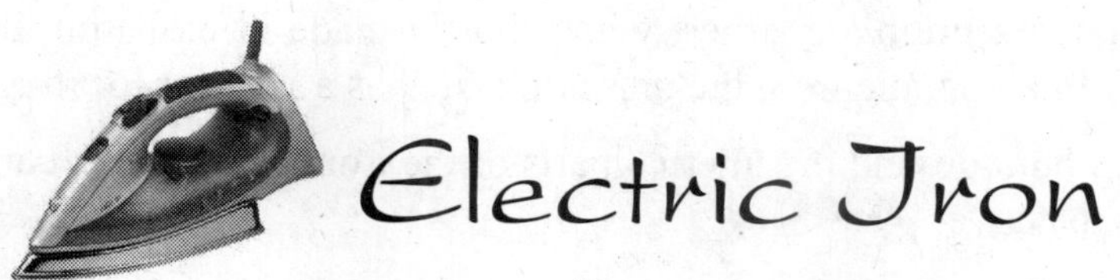

Electric Iron

It was long well-known that combination of heat and pressure can iron out wrinkles and even bring proper creases to the dresses, but a real iron took a long time to evolve. We have again come along way with automatic irons and steam irons[20]. It takes the help of the heating effect of electricity. There are basically two types of electric irons: Non-automatic and automatic. As the name suggests the automatic iron regulates temperature to suit the fabric. A domestic iron consists of quite a few interesting parts.

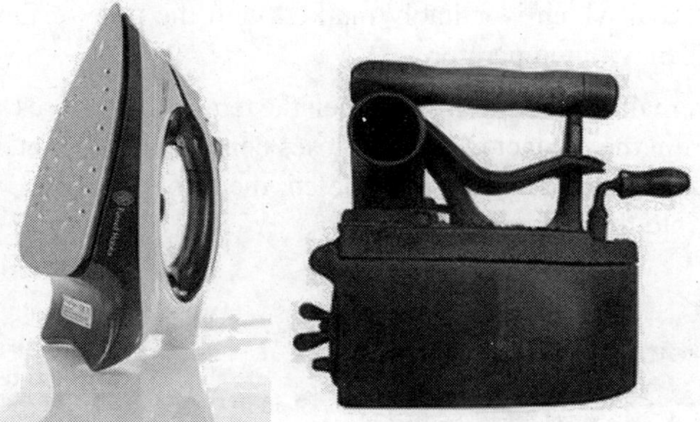

Heating Element: Mica is the very best non-conductor of heat and electricity. So, it is a very good insulating material which can also withstand very high temperatures. As already discussed nichrome wire is coiled around a sheet of mica with some more mica covering it on both sides as an insulator. The two ends of the nichrome wire are connected to the contact strips. The entire assembly is riveted together to make it robust. This heating assembly is bolted and pressed hard between the sole plate and pressure plate. The cover, handle are built around and the terminals are taken out.

When electrically powered, the heating element gets heated up and conducts the heat to the sole plate. Asbestos sheets are used on the top of this assembly to prevent heat spreading to the cover and the top of the iron.

Sole Plate: The sole plate is the thick, triangular-shaped slab is of cast iron over which the electric iron is built up. Its bottom surface used for ironing, which is heavily chromium plated, to give polished surface for ironing and also to prevent it from rusting. Presently in better models, the bottoms are teflon coated. Incidentally, the teflon coated ones are lighter and easier to handle.

20 In China around 1st century BC, metal pans filled with hot water were used for smoothing fabrics. By 17th century thick delta-shaped slabs of cast iron, with a handle were used after heating in a fire. Rudimentary model was invented in 1882 by Henry W. Seeley, a New York inventor, who patented his 'Electric flatiron' on June 6, 1882. His iron weighed almost 15 pounds and took a long time to warm up.

Pressure Plate: The pressure plate is heavy and mostly made of cast iron. It holds the heating element in position. In automatic iron, the pressure plate has a hole for locating the thermostat.

Cover : The cover is built around the internal parts of the iron. The handle, connectors and mains wire are attached to the cover plate.

Handle: Bakelite is choice material as the handle as it is resistant to heat and keeps it cool.

Then how do we control the temperature of an automatic iron?

Thermostat: For maintaining the optimum temperature, a thermostat is used with a pilot lamp serving as an indicator. Thermostat works on the principle of expansion of metals. Metals expand as the temperature raises and different metals expand differently. Thermostat is a bimetallic strip consisting of two different metals bonded together. They have a different coefficient of expansion. If such a strip is heated, it starts to curve towards the metal which has less expansion. On cooling, it returns to the normal position. Contact points are attached to this strip and a spring strip to act like a switch. A small cam is fixed to shift the contact point. The cam in turn is connected to a temperature control dial which is suitably marked with the type of fabric, silk, 'wool', 'cotton', 'linen', etc. rather than with temperature.

The contact points remain closed normally. When the temperature raises significantly, the bimetallic strip curves away from the contact points and loses contact, thereby interrupting the power supply. Heating is temporarily stopped. When it is cooled, the bimetallic strip returns making the contact again. Please look into the following figures.

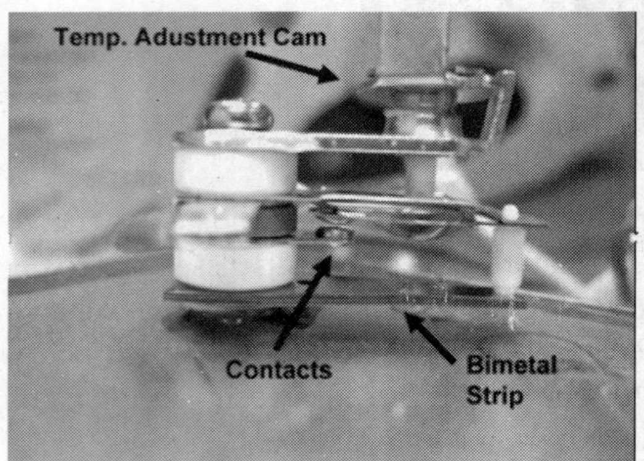

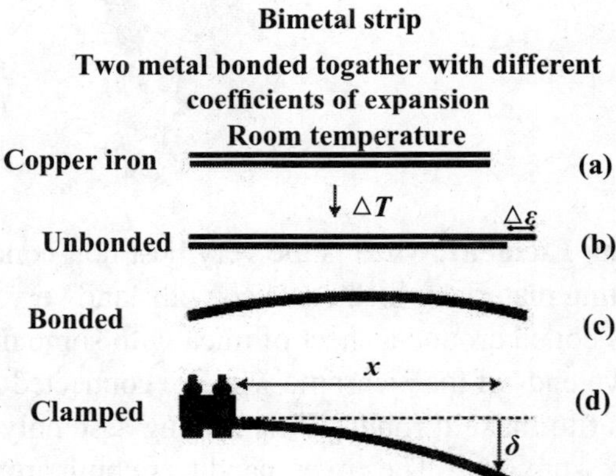

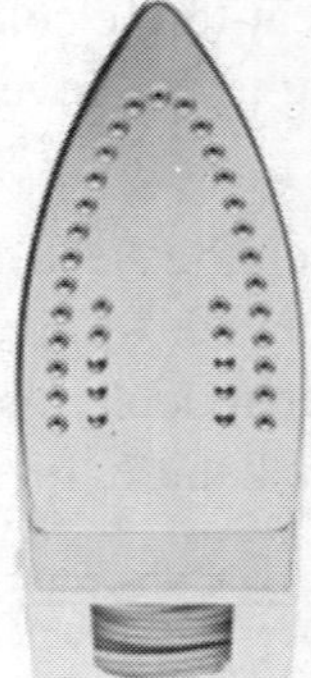

Pilot Lamp: The pilot lamp is placed in series with the thermostat which indicates on-off condition of the iron.

Steam Iron: Then while ironing, we often sprinkle water on to the cloth to take out the wrinkles out easily. Why not automate it? Result- Steam Iron!

Steam iron has a small water reservoir, push button to start jets of steam and steam nozzles on the sole plate. The push button can select constant steam, jets of steam, etc. which directly spray onto the cloth. When steam button is pressed, the water goes down into the nozzles, turns into steam. Does a great job of removing wrinkles! But of late simple automatic iron is preferred over the steam irons, because of the problem of clogging vents.

Care and Tips

- ✓ Maintain a clean iron to speed up the process of ironing clothes and make it smoother. Keep the sole plate polished and shining always.
- ✓ Cleaning a hot iron is dangerous. If waxy or oily substance is struck, heat it at maximum setting and run it across newspaper until the residue disappears.
- ✓ Do not use a screw driver or knife to clean the sole plate; you will end up scratching it. Scratched iron will never give good results.
- ✓ Do not let power cord dangle. If it touches, hot iron will burn the wire and insulation.

Geysers

If you're bothered about stress and tense muscles, a hot shower is the answer. It relaxes, rejuvenates and improves our reflexes. It soothes our nerves, promotes blood circulation and washes away allergens. Hot water bath sanitizes and improves our personal hygiene.

Water is traditionally heated in a vessel on a stove and carried to the bath room. We often insert a finger in the water to check how hot that is. But clearly it is not safe as there is a possibility of water spillage while transporting. Also we can heat only a limited quantity and take it by turns, which is tedious and time consuming. Unfortunately, it takes a lot of energy and time to heat water. You know that when you are waiting for bucket of water to get hot on a stove. Rich and mighty, of course had those enormous copper boilers in the back yard which were heated by logs of wood.

Then, we have the immersion rod which was hanged into a bucket of water. They are portable, cheap and can be used anywhere without any additional fixtures. They are helpful but could prove to be unsafe, particularly poor quality ones. Heating is not uniform as the heating is done through convection. They are not automatic; so you have to put your finger to check how hot the water is. Make sure to remove the wall plug before you do that!

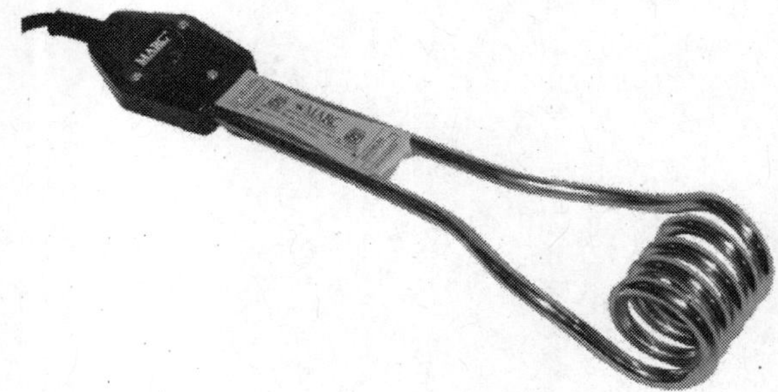

That brings us to the geysers[21] or hot water heaters. Most of them are electric while in the foreign countries gas is also used. Then, we have two types of them, storage type or the so-called instant heater. Insulated nichrom wire does the heating job. Nichrom offers great resistance to electricity and in the process heats up. Water surrounds a coil with insulated heating wire inside (called the heating element) and the water gets hot. A thermostat (read chapter on electric iron) senses the temperature and stops heating when the set point is reached and starts again when the temperature falls below. Lights indicate power on, heating on conditions. Additionally, a small safety valve is incorporated in the system which relieves the pressure and temperature if they go off beyond a certain limit. These are basics of any electric geyser and all these are enclosed in a container.

21 Benjamin Waddy Maughan a painter invented the first instantaneous domestic water heater that didn't use solid fuel in London, England, in 1868. It was named 'Geyser' after an Icelandic gushing hot spring.

In the reservoir or storage type you have a water tank with a heating element inside. Cold water is released into it from the bottom to make sure that the tank is always full and hot water is taken off from the top. Tank is insulated and thermostat keeps the temperature constant.

Tankless geysers or instant geysers heat water directly without the use of a storage tank. When cold water let in, it travels through a pipe into the heater. The electric element heats the water and hot water flows out. The geyser delivers a constant supply of hot water and you need not to wait for a storage tank to fill up with enough hot water. But its flow rate is limited, say 7 to 15 litres and at higher rates, water just passes without heating.

So now which one is good?: If demand for hot water is large, storage type is the choice. But they are not energy efficient as there is a standby loss. Greater quantity of water is heated whether you use it or not. A tankless water heater, heats water only when it is being used. So, the energy is consumed only when you are using it. ENERGY STAR qualified tankless water heater consumes still less power.

Storage type geyser requires more space and more elaborate plumbing, but instant water heater is compact and takes up less space.

Storage type heater can store up to 150 litres of hot water and can fulfil all the demands of kitchen, bathroom, and laundry. But instant water heater can only supply a few litres of hot water at a time.

Some interesting features are built into water heaters like digital controls, remote control, self - cleaning units and automatic shut off valves. Stainless steel housing, higher pressure rating, better insulation and special polymer coatings increase their life. In some models, heating elements are built into the showerheads. Star rated geysers consume less power.

Induction water heaters are also coming up on the horizon. Instead of direct heating, this technology creates a magnetic field within the geyser and makes the best of it in the heating process. It is estimated this method can save 30% of the time and 60% power consumption in heating water and also save installation space. So select a geyser which actually suits your needs and saves on the power bill. But the bottom line is save water and save power. Here, are some tips to do it.

Heating Tips

- ✓ Set the thermostat on your water heater to minimum. There is no point in keeping high and adding cold water afterwards in the bucket or in the wall mixer. 50°C is comfortable.
- ✓ Repair leaky taps and faucets promptly; a leaky tap loses a lot of litres in wastage. Water build-up in or around geyser may indicate a leak.
- ✓ Insulate your geysers and careful not to cover the thermostat.
- ✓ Insulate the hot water pipe and insulate cold water pipe until your reach.
- ✓ Buy energy saving and water-saving model to save power and water.
- ✓ Drain some water once in every 3 months to remove scaling or foreign particles. They can restrict heat transfer and brings down the efficiency of your geyser. It is a good practice to service the water heater once in two years and one year in case of hard water. Its efficiency will definitely improve if the scaling on the heating element is removed.

Safety

- ✓ Wiring of the heater is important. Old aluminium wires, loose connections, bad installation can be dangerous.
- ✓ Geysers can explode if the water gets overheated or the thermostat does not work properly. A safety relief valve is installed on the geyser to relieve excess pressure. Do not remove it or bypass it.
- ✓ Hot water can cause serious burns. Human skin can scald in less than 5 seconds at 60°C, but a little slower at 53°C. Please be careful while carrying hot water or mixing it.
- ✓ That brings us to the next point. Some bacteria particularly Legionella incubates well in water less than 55°C. So, balance the scalding risk and bacteria risk by setting the thermostat to 55°C.
- ✓ In case of an emergency: switch off the geyser, turn off the water supply and if necessary, drain water from the heater.
- ✓ Geysers should necessarily be always full. If not, the heating coil may burnout.

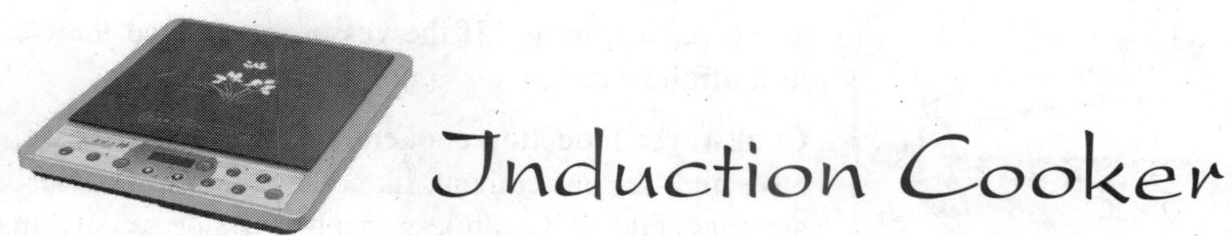

Induction Cooker

Induction cookers are adorning more and more modern kitchens. Other forms of cooking use fuel such as wood, coal or gas, or heat is generated by electric heater, which are all indirect heating methods. But in induction cooking, heat is generated directly in the cooking vessel. It is fast, efficient and economical.

Design: Here is an inside view of an induction cooker: large copper coil which create the magnetic field, cooling fan below it, power supply and control circuits are around.

Right below the cooking surface, a powerful high-frequency electromagnet is sealed. Electronics in the cooker sense if the vessel is magnetic or not, sufficient size or not, then lock and start the process. When a cast iron or steel vessel is placed on it, electromagnetism is induced into it, by the associated electronics. An alternating electric current flows through the coil, which produces an oscillating magnetic field. While the current is large, it is produced by a low voltage. This creates an electric current called eddy current in it, which moves along the surface of the vessel. By the surface resistance of the vessel, heat is generated directly in the pot or pan itself. The internal circuitry can instantaneously control the power, heat, temperature, and timing of the cooking process. The unit can detect whether a magnetic cookware is present or not and automatically turn it off when cookware is removed from it.

In effect the electronics circuits of the heater power a coil with a high frequency voltage which produces corresponding high-frequency electromagnetic field.

That electromagnetic field penetrates cooking vessel if it is made up of magnetic material such as iron. This creates an alternating electric current, which in turn generates heat which is transferred to the food in the vessel.

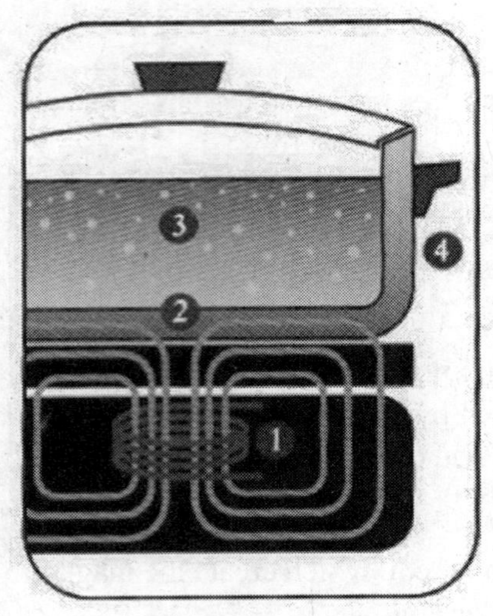

If the vessel is not electromagnetic, the circuit cannot couple and gives a warning. If the vessel is removed the electronics turn off the current.

Cookware: Induction cookers work well with vessels which have high ferrous content, like cast iron or mild steel and thus are magnetic. All stainless steels are not readily magnetic. Stainless steel pans will work if at least the base is a magnetic. If a magnet sticks well to the bottom of it, the vessel will work. Aluminium or copper vessels do not work, so also glass and ceramics[22].

Pros and Cons: Induction cooking is miles[23] ahead in efficiency of gas cooking. While the energy-efficiency values of induction-cookers range from 83% to 90%, while those for gas cooking are around 55% to 30%. The induction effect does not heat the air around the vessel, saving loss of heat. An induction cooker can boil water through several layers of paper. Cooking is faster and there are no open flames. In normal operation, the cooking surface stays cool enough to touch after the cooking vessel is removed. Heating shuts down as soon as the vessel is removed.

The greatest drawback of induction cooking is that it only works with cooking vessels made of magnetic materials. Steel is strong, but poor conductor of heat; aluminium and copper are better, but are soft. Why not combine them? Now, we have sandwiched vessels, the outermost layer is magnetic stainless steel[24] and the middle layer is aluminium or copper to improve heat conduction. The inner layer is full corrosion resistant stainless steel, or steel lined with PTFE (polytetrafluoroethylene), better known as Teflon®. However, feverish research is on to allow use of any metal cookware, copper and aluminium.

Cast iron is still good, and if it is silken smooth, it is the original 'non-stick' cookware. Modern cookers offer a number of user-friendly features like touch control and pre-set menus by digital display. Timers can be set up to 24 hours, and they also have countdown timers. Most of them have a temperature range of 70° C to 270° C. Wattage can be set from 120W to 2000W. Cookers can sense the vessel presence and shut off automatically if the vessel is removed. They will start only if a magnetic vessel of sufficient size is placed on the stove and also caution if they are not.

Care and Tips

✓ Do not place packed food in aluminium foils to reheat. Aluminium foil can melt and can crack the top.

22 A higher surface resistance produces more heat for similar currents. Aluminium or copper cookware is more conductive than steel, and offer less surface resistance. Less resistance produces less heat. The induction cooker will not work efficiently with such pots.

23 Though first patents date from the early 1900s, practical demonstrations of induction stoves were made around mid-1950s by the Frigidaire division of General Motors. The cooker was shown heating a pot of water with a newspaper placed between the stove and the cooking vessel. Westinghouse Electric Corporation displayed their prototype at the 1971 National Association of Home Builders convention in Houston, Texas.

24 Steel is iron with a slight (c. 1%) admixture of carbon, which changes the qualities of the iron. Stainless steel is steel with some chromium alloyed with the steel; if the chromium content is at least 12%, the alloy qualifies as 'stainless' steel, but 18% chromium is the norm. It is thus '18/10' stainless steel.

- ✓ The cooktop surface is 'ceramic glass', which is very strong, tolerates very high temperatures and sudden temperature changes. But if a cookware is dropped on it, it may crack the ceramic top.
- ✓ Do not slide vessels on its surface as they can scratch. Do not scratch any part of the Induction Cooker with sharp objects.
- ✓ These cookers should never be used with empty vessels.
- ✓ Do not leave an Induction Cooker unattended for a very long time.
- ✓ Please do not keep these cookers on metal platforms or on metal plates as the induction may lock on to them rather than the vessel.
- ✓ Keep the cooker away from gas stove.
- ✓ Do not splash water on to it or clean it with water.
- ✓ Adequate ventilation is always necessary for all cooking particularly so for induction cooking.

Automatic Electric Rice Cooker

Rice had been staple food in the Asian countries and is traditionally used in Indian homes from times immemorial. India has the largest paddy output and is also the fourth largest exporter of rice in the world. Many festivals in India are associated with the harvest of paddy such as *Sankranthi* in Andhra Pradesh, *Makara Sankranthi* in Karnataka, *Thai Pongal* in Tamil Nadu, *Onam* in Kerala, *Bihu* in Assam, *Nabanna* in West Bengal. Given a very large varieties of rice. Cooking rice is an art. My wife does all the cooking; I do eating. I could not master making good rice. A new daughter-in-law into a household was never able to cook rice properly, either it became a paste or too hard to eat. Mother-in-laws took pride in teaching that girl a skill to add appropriate amount of water, heat at right temperature and remove at the right time.

Then came the electric rice cooker! Japanese were first of course[25].

Thanks to these rice cookers, even I can cook rice in less than 30 minutes. I can also cook a variety of rice recipes such as *pongal, biryani* and even *idlis*. They do not speed up cooking but can cook better. You can attend to other household works while it is cooking. When the rice is fully cooked, the cooker stops main heating, thus preventing the rice from being overcooked but keeps the rice warm.

25 In 1945, the Mitsubishi Electric Corporation of Japan introduced electric rice cooker, though it was not automatic. The first practical electric rice cooker was invented by Toshiba Electric Corporation in association with Yoshitada Minami. In December 1956, Toshiba presented the first commercial automated electric rice cookers on the market. But then, a ceramic rice steamer dated to 1250 BC is on display in the British Museum.

The cooking bowl in the cooker is generally removable. Right below it is the heater and thermostat. A spring keeps the thermostat in good thermal contact with the bowl. You can keep the rice and water in separate bowl but you should add some more water into the main bowl until the separator is just immersed. Add the right amount of water to the required rice quantity. Now pull the switch to cooking so that the rice/water mixture is heated at full power. As long as there is water in the pan, the temperature should be stable. When the water reaches its boiling point of 100°C; it can't get hotter. When the water gets evaporated, or when it is absorbed by the rice, the temperature will increase. Bimetallic thermostat under the pan detects this and switches of the main heating. Most of the cookers now switch over to warming mode of about 65°C.

Heating element

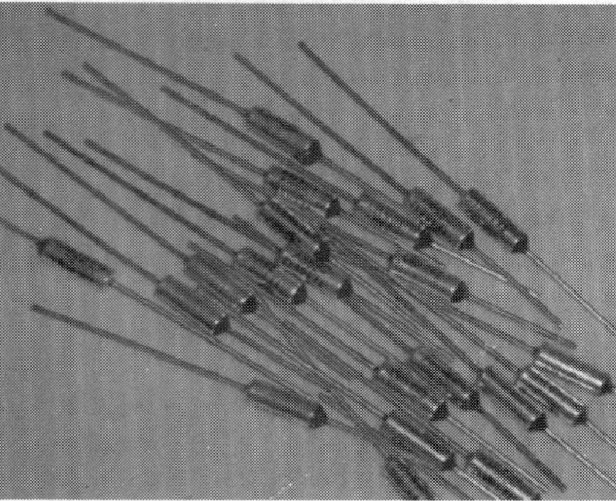

Temperature sensing elements

There are some simple tips if you want fluffy rice in a jiffy.

- ✓ Any experienced lady or cook will tell you that the actual amount of water to be used depends on the type, age and storage conditions of the rice. You may experiment a little in the beginning.
- ✓ Do not be childish. Do not open the lid while it is cooking just to watch how it is cooking. Opening disturbs the steaming process, upsets moisture distribution and of course cools the process.
- ✓ Keep cooked rice in the cooker until use. Though, it can keep it hot for several hours, the longer it is kept warmed, the more taste will be lost.
- ✓ If you stir rice while it's cooking, you are about making it suitable as substitute paste.
- ✓ To test rice, take a grain and pinch it between your fingers. If it's hard or if the inside is white in color, then it's definitely not cooked. As the saying goes only one grain is enough.
- ✓ Sometimes a teaspoon or two of pure vegetable cooking oil into the rice will help keep the grains from lumping together.

Microwave Cooking

21st century has changed our style of living, improved our standard of living and altered our thinking mechanism. New products are continuously added which make our kitchen life more comfortable and convenient. The housewife or the cook is no longer glued to the kitchen floor. From the war front, microwaves entered our kitchens, result of extreme engineering walking to our homes.

Microwaves have many useful applications from radars to telephone, radio and television communications. They are also used to detect speeding cars, treat muscle soreness, and cure plywood, and rubber plus a host of other uses. Microwave ovens are now used for defrosting, reheating, and cooking. Microwave ovens offer automatic defrosting and a range of pre-programmed and programmable power and time settings for various food items. But its use in the kitchen had interesting beginning. Use of microwaves for domestic cooking came by accident[26].

A Little Bit about Waves: Before we talk about microwave ovens, a little bit about waves. We are surrounded by electromagnetic waves which include the visible light, radio waves, X-rays and gamma rays, etc. Here is picture of electromagnetic spectrum. You may compare the sizes.

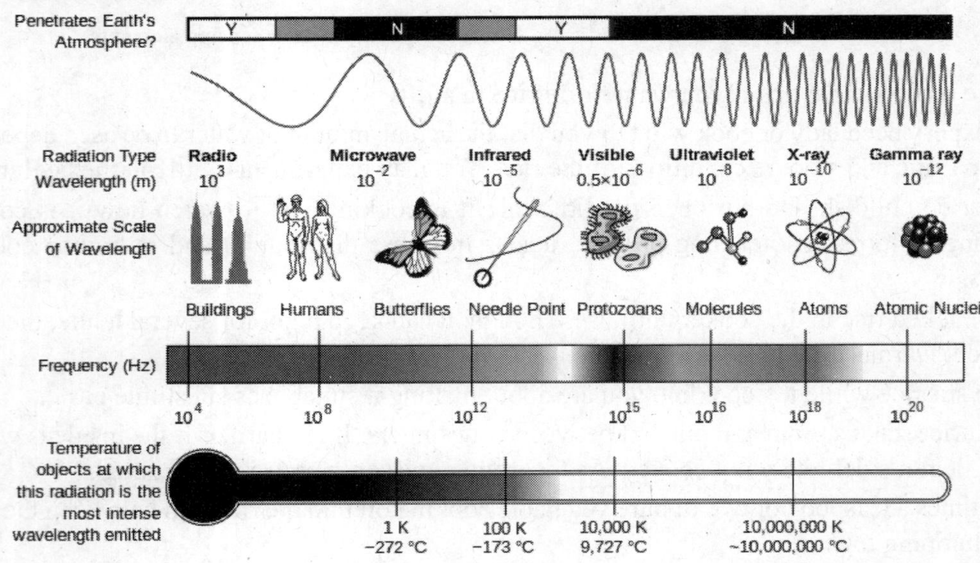

26 One day, while Dr. Perry. L. Spencer was touring his laboratory in Raytheon, he stood in front of a magnetron. He felt a sudden sensation on his body. He soon realized that the chocolate bar in his pocket got melted down. He suspected that the microwaves from the magnetron melted the chocolate as the body heat could not have done it. The next day he put an egg near the magnetron, which soon began to tremor and quake. Just as a curious colleague moved closer to get a better view, the egg exploded and splashed hot yoke all over his face.
It became clear that the microwaves are agitating the water molecules in the chocolate and in the process heating it. It will be interesting to note that the first microwave used to weigh about 750 lb and 5.5 feet high.

Microwaves are in the frequency range of 300 to 300,000 mega hertz (MHz) (million cycles per second). They can pass through materials like glass, paper, plastic and ceramic, but are reflected by metals. When these waves meet water molecules, they agitate them, thereby producing heat thus leading to temperature rise. Hence, they directly heat the food inside rather than by indirect heating like electric or gas cooking.

So we need a magnetron which can generate microwave frequencies, direct and distribute them onto the food, necessary power supply, control circuit and a suitable housing that contains these waves inside and prevents them from escaping. Modern microwave cookers are fairly sophisticated offering a number of useful features in user friendly displays, timing, temperature, etc.

A microwave oven consists of:

- Power supply and a high voltage transformer, which passes energy to the magnetron
- A magnetron control circuit (usually with a microcontroller)
- A cavity magnetron
- A waveguide, and
- A cooking chamber.

Power Supply and Control Circuit: Domestic power supply is made suitable for the microprocessor control circuit and for the magnetron. The circuit has a number of safety features also built into it, like child locks, door locks.

Main Circuit Board and Microcontroller: It is an integrated circuit which controls all the operations of the cooker.

Transformer: Magnetron needs a high voltage in the order of 4000 volts for which a step-up transformer is used. A transformer has two or more windings which can increase (step-up) or decrease the voltage (step-down) by magnetic coupling.

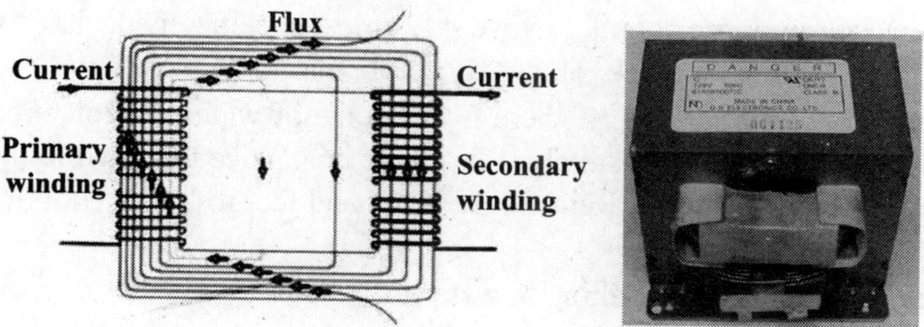

Magnetron: It is a vacuum tube which generates high frequency (2450 MHz) electromagnetic field which is directed into the cooker by an antenna and wave guide.

Waveguide: It is a rectangular metal tube which serves a very essential function of directing microwaves into the cooking cavity and prevents their escape.

Cooking Cavity: It is the place where you keep the food. However, microwaves do enter irregularly and scatter randomly. So 'cold spots' can occur in micro-waved food. So, stirrer or turntables are used. If food is not cooked evenly, bacteria survive.

Stirrer: It allows more uniform heating of food by evenly distributing microwaves in the food.

Turntable: It rotates the food around in the microwave cavity to expose them uniformly to microwaves.

Cooking Chamber: It is a specially made metallic container which will not allow any microwaves to escape known as a Faraday Cage which traps the microwaves inside the box, so that they cook the food and not things around the microwave oven, like you. Even the door is microwave proof, though light can pass through. It has a fine mesh through which light can pass but not microwaves. Because the size of the perforations in the mesh is much less than the wavelength of microwaves, they cannot pass through, while visible light (with a much shorter wavelength) can.

A typical consumer microwave oven may consume up to 1100 W of electricity while developing 700 W of microwave power, at the efficiency rate of 64%. Microwave ovens come in different

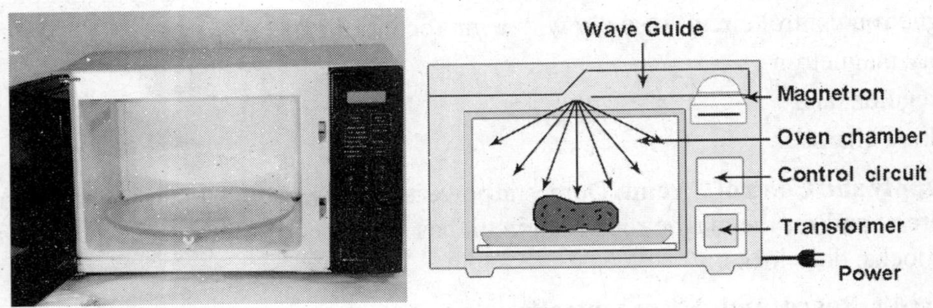

sizes and designs. When you want to buy one, buy the right size, suitable to your cooking needs. Microwave ovens are quite safe; however, you take some basic safety precautions.

- ✓ Metal vessels and glass containers with designs are not suitable to be placed inside a microwave. They can create sparks and metallic forks are particularly susceptible.
- ✓ Most of the plastic containers are not microwave safe unless specifically declared so. Do not use anything and everything in microwave. They may spark, burn, and blow out.
- ✓ Microwaves heat water; nothing else. If there is any trace of water or moisture in the plastic or glass vessel, it gets hot; hence not suitable. To check this, place the bowl in the cooker with water and microwave it for a minute. Remove the bowl and feel it. If it is cool, it is microwave safe.
- ✓ Rice and Dal are best cooked after soaking in water for at least 20 minutes.
- ✓ Before cooking potatoes, tomatoes, pierce them all over so that they don't blast.
- ✓ Always allow 2-5 minutes standing time for food cooked in microwave prior to consumption.
- ✓ Microwave ovens work with really very high voltages in the order of 25000V. Do not ever try to repair it yourself.
- ✓ There are several safety devices and interlocks are provided in these cookers. Never bypass them.

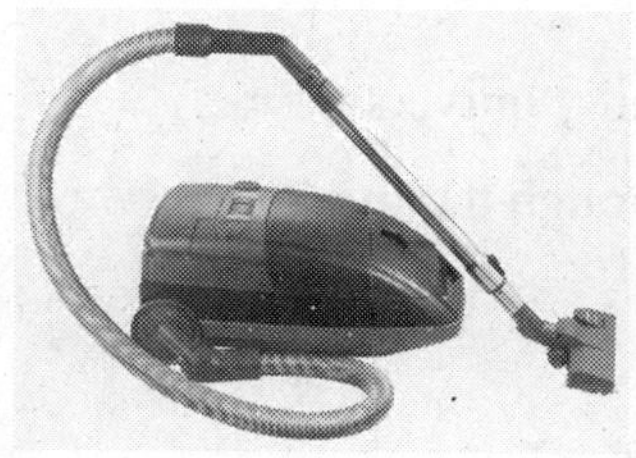

Vacuum Cleaner

Indian homes started using vacuum cleaners in a large way, because non-availability of housemaids, faster life styles and aggressive domestic marketing. Vacuum cleaners keep our home clean and free from dust mites.

Vacuum cleaner[27] sucks up dust and dirt from floors, or other surfaces, by creating a partial vacuum at the inlet. The dirt is collected by a dust bag which was later disposed off. It is a simple machine composed of a few essential components.

An inlet port is the place where extension hoses and specialised attachments like, tools, brushes and extension wands are connected. Extension hoses naturally extend the reach, while specialised attachments allow them to reach otherwise inaccessible places or clean a variety of surfaces. Some of them are:

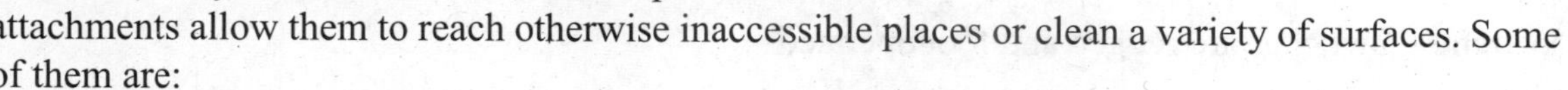

- Hard floor brush
- Carpeted floor brush
- Dusting brush;
- Crevice tool;
- Upholstery tool.

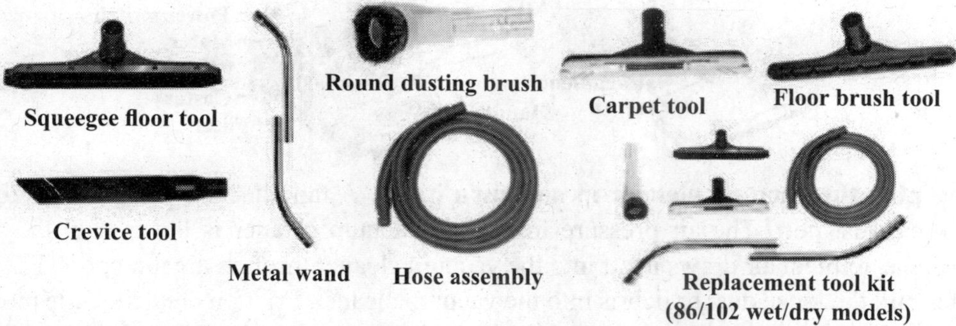

27 Daniel Hess invented a vacuum cleaner in 1860 in America, calling it a carpet sweeper. His machine however, had a rotating brush. While on a train ride, Hubert Cecil Booth got an idea, placed a handkerchief across his mouth and started sucking air. This action pulled lot of dust onto the handkerchief, making clear that vacuum could capture dust. He patented a vacuum cleaner driven by an oil engine in 1901. It was monstrous machine which was called 'Puffing Billy.'

The basic parts of a vacuum cleaner are:

Electric motor - A fan is coupled to an electric motor (generally universal type.)

Fan- Fan creates the vacuum to pull the dust into the hose through the inlet port.

Porous bag- The dust collected is let into this bag.

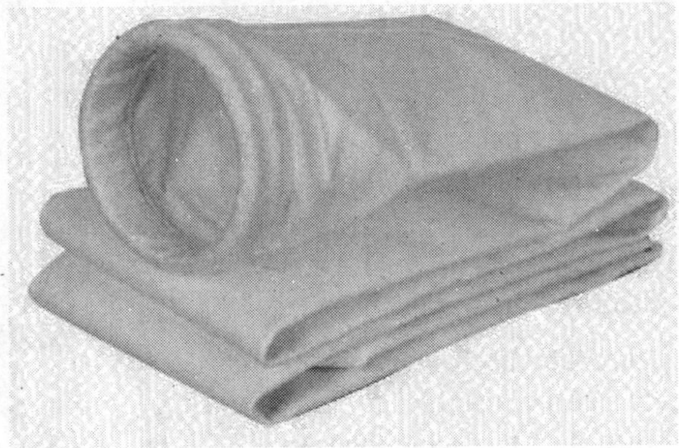

Porous bag

Exhaust port- Only air goes out of here after filtering through the bag.

Cable winder- Vacuum cleaners have normally long mains cables to be able to reach far off places. The cable can be drawn back into the machine by a pressing the cable winder built into the machine.

Switches- Switches are rugged and foot operated.

Housing – It contains all these components except the vacuum hoses and fittings.

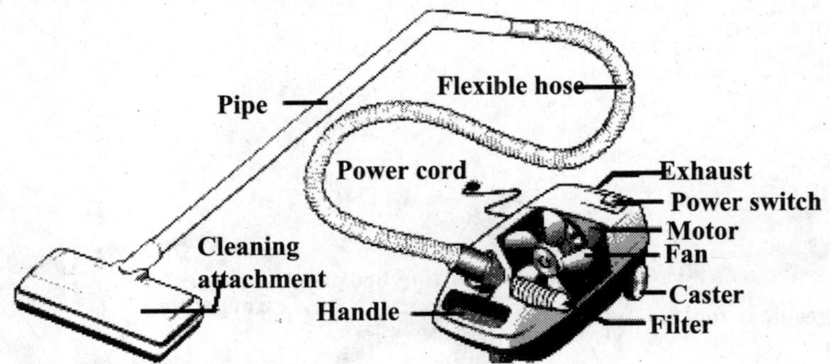

When you plug the vacuum cleaner in and turn it on: A fan attached to the motor forces air toward the exhaust port. The air pressure inside the vacuum cleaner is lower than the pressure outside. So, the ambient air draws itself into the vacuum cleaner through the inlet port. The moving air particles pull the loose dust or debris into the vacuum cleaner. Friction created while moving the brushes releases the dirt and debris. It is readily picked up by the suction air stream. Some vacuum cleaners have rotating brushes which release the dust and dirt.

Then the dusty air passes through a porous bag, before it is exhausted. This bag acts as an air filter. These bags are porous with tiny holes which allow air particles to pass but would not let dirt particles to pass through. Thus, the dirt and debris collect in the bag. When the bag is full, an indication lights up on the vacuum cleaner. The suction is lost and vacuum cleaner would no longer be efficient. It is time to remove the bag, dispose it off and fix a new one.

Taking on this basic idea, a wide range of vacuum cleaners in a variety of sizes and models are developed — small battery-operated hand-held devices, to domestic and central vacuum cleaners. Modern vacuum cleaners can also be used as blowers. They have interesting attachments to make it a sprayer.

Care and Tips: While it looks like a simple machine, the machine can lose its vacuum, even a simple twist of the suction hose, which often happens. When the motor suddenly speeds up or whirrs faster, you know the hose is twisted and lost suction.

We'll look at a few of the factors that determine suction power.

✓ We have seen that the dust gets collected in the bag. When the bag gets filled up by the dust the machine loses suction. So, replace the bag. It is also possible to clean the bag but be careful.

✓ Similarly if there is a hole or crack in the suction hose, the machine loses its vacuum.

✓ Narrower vacuum pickups can suck heavier dirt particles than wider attachments, because they can develop a stronger suction force.

Electric Chimneys

A kitchen is where the lady of the house spends most of her time. A lady guest walking into a house would invariably like to see the kitchen first and how beautiful it is kept. We generally keep our drawing room inviting, but forget the kitchen.

Electric chimneys are no longer an adornment. Until recently simple exhaust fan was trying its best to suck the fumes. Indian food is very aromatic and creates a lot of fumes. An exhaust fan removes the fumes but not before they enter your eyes. So, if you want a smoke free kitchen, if your cooking involves a lot of frying and your eyes are sensitive to fumes, electric chimney is a better choice. However the noise level is high, more than in an exhaust fan.

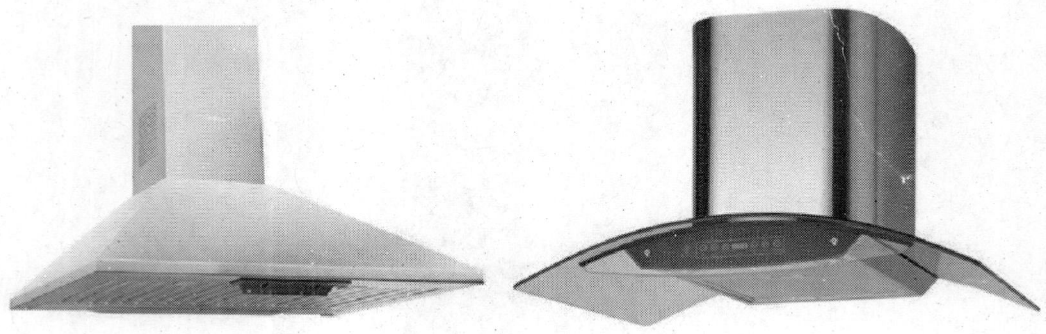

Kitchen chimney is similar to a vacuum cleaner except for few differences. There is the motor and blower which sucks the air from over the stove. It is the reverse of a domestic fan except that it has more suction capacity. Filters trap the oil and fumes, just like dust bag in the vacuum cleaner. Then the oil-free air is directed out through ducting or hose or PVC pipe.

But a few important features need to be kept in mind while buying an electric chimney apart from just the sizes, 60 cm and 90 cm.

Air Suction Capacity – The blower's capacity to suck odors and oily vapors is measured in cubic meters per hour (m^3/hr). While for normal cooking, medium air suction capacity of about 400 m^3/hr would suffice but for heavy cooking such as non-vegetarian food or deep frying, suction more than above 400 m^3/hr would be ideal.

Number of blowers – The more number of blowers, the more effective would be the removal of unwanted smells, oil and grease.

Filters – There are several types of filters, mesh filters, baffle filters and charcoal filters. Baffle filters are considered to be better than the mesh filters in terms of Indian cooking style.

Ductings- After the particles of oil and grease, etc., are trapped in the baffle/mesh filter, and the fumes are removed out of the house by ducting PVC pipe or hose is used for this purpose. You may need to make a hole in the wall for this. You may route it through the exhaust fan holes after removing it. Do not use a smaller size piping.

Filters: The aluminium mesh filter consists of a multi-layer meshes for effective purification. Each mesh contains tiny holes, where the masala and oil particles present in the fumes are trapped. This filter can be washed easily either by hand or in a dishwasher. But then these small particles can also cling into the mesh holes, coating and blocking the filters, thereby impede their very purpose. Unfortunately, Indian food is not only spicy but also greasy and oily.

A development on the mesh filters is the baffle filters. Series of overlapped baffles trap and separate oil molecules and spices from the fumes. They do not block the suction. Baffle filters are almost 30 per cent more effective than mesh filters. They are made of stainless steel or aluminium and stainless steel is stronger while aluminium is lighter. So, cleaning baffle filter chimneys is quite easy.

Mesh filter

Baffle filter

Charcoal or activated carbon filters are available in certain models at extra cost, excellent in removing the odour. There are used in recycling mode. Oil, grease and spices are trapped in the baffle or mesh filter and the fumes are filtered through the activated carbon filter. The clean, odourless air is then circulated into the room.

Auto Clean Chimneys: Auto clean chimneys are next level of kitchen convenience. Instead of the necessity of removing the filters, cleaning them and fixing them, the entire process is automatic. A small little pot with a pump is built into the chimney. Pour soapy water into the pot and start auto

cleaning. The pump starts cleaning the internals. After cleaning, the soapy water collects in a tray and the oil is collected in the bowls under the blowers. Tray and bowls can be easily removed and contents dispensed with.

A Few Tips to Remember:

- ✓ Cleaning is a must depending upon the filter design of the chimney and kitchen use. Mesh filters should be washed in warm detergent water every 8-10 days, while baffle filters may require cleaning every 2-3 weeks. Charcoal filters may need change every 3-4 months.
- ✓ Install the chimney at an appropriate height as recommended by the manufacturer. Most recommend a height of 60 cm from the stove.
- ✓ It should be accessible for cleaning.
- ✓ Do not compromise on the exhaust ducting. Do not use size lesser than the exhaust hole in the chimney. Do not make sharp bends.

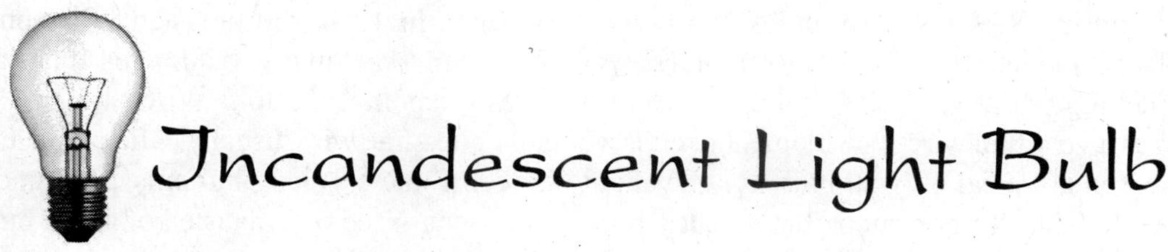

Incandescent Light Bulb

What a light bulb? That glows with a flick of a switch! An article on that light bulb? Ooops...

- Do you know that the inside temperature of a simple light bulb is in the order of 2500°C?
- Do you know that the temperature on the glass of that simple light bulb is in the order of 250°C?
- Do you know that simple light bulb is filled with rare gases?
- Do you know that the filament inside that simple light bulb is about two meters long?
- And the inventor tried about 2500 different materials to get the right material for the filament.
- And that simple light bulb that has become part of our lives is about 100 years old!
- And is just on its way out.

Ladies and gentlemen, that bulb is not simple bulb!!!

It's much more than what we see everywhere. It has got a cherished history [28]. It is made out of thin glass. Inside the glass is filled with gases like argon and nitrogen. At the centre is a coiled coil of thin wire of tungsten connected to two lead wires that come out as terminals sealed without air or gas leaks. Push it into its holder by a twist. Switch on. Electricity instantly heats tungsten filament up about 2,500 degrees Celsius and bathes the room with white light in a process called incandescence.

They do not need additional fittings, are cheap and also work well with AC or DC. So, we use them everywhere, home to cars to decoration to advertisement. They are even deliberately used for heating in certain applications. Fortunately, these bulbs emit light with colour that's almost natural.

They are available in variety of sizes, shapes, wattages, in voltages from 1.5 volts to about 300 volts and are sold by the electrical power consumed in watts and working voltage. Power ratings range from about 0.1 watt to about 10,000 watts. However, these incandescent bulbs are very sensitive to voltage fluctuations.

28 In 1810, Davy demonstrated to the Royal Institution the first arc lamp using charcoal rods. In 1840, British Astronomer and Chemist, Warren de la Rue created the world's first light bulb, with platinum coil in a vacuum tube– 40 years before Edison. Joseph Swan, a British physicist and chemist worked with carbonized paper filaments in evacuated glass bulb by 1850. He lit his house with light bulb for the first time in the world. Thomas Edison's first successful test was on 22 October 1879 when the bulb lasted 13.5 hours. His later experiments with carbonized bamboo filament lasted over 1200 hours.

Introduced in 1879, the early bulbs had carbon filaments. In 1906, the tungsten[29] filament was introduced and marketed by Tungsram in Hungary. Tungsten filament can last longer. It has a very high melting point of 3422°C, while the bulb operates at about 1750 to 3000°C. It can also be drawn as a very thin wire. The filament itself is a coil of coiled fine wire, usually called 'coiled coil.' Filament in a typical 60-watt bulb may be about 6.5 feet (2 meters) long but only one-hundredth of an inch thick. To prevent oxidation early bubs were vacuumised or exhausted of all air but now they are filled with an inert gas such as argon (93%) and nitrogen (7%) or sometimes krypton.

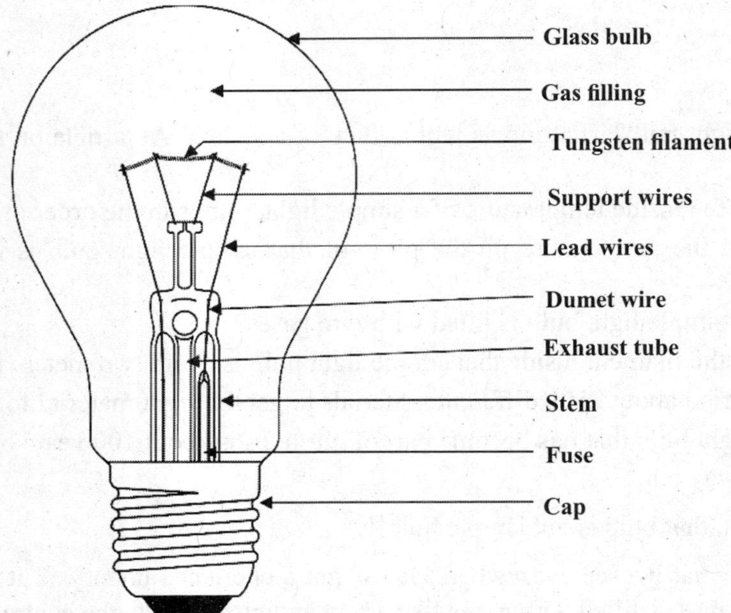

There are two types of bases or caps, screwed or bayonet, but the higher wattage bulbs have screw base. In some cases the cap is also used as contact point, like in the case of automobile bulbs. Most of the automobile headlight bulbs have two filaments in one glass enclosure. The filaments share a common contact point in the cap, and can be lit separately or together. Most of the light bulbs have clear glasses, but some have frosted glasses. Frosted bulbs diffuse the light, so that the lighting is not harsh. They are coated inside with kaolin.

A normal light bulb lasts about 750 to 1,000 hours in normal use[30]. Unfortunately, 90% of the power consumed by an incandescent light bulb is lost as heat. In the process, tungsten filament evaporates, which then breaks, and the bulb 'burns out.' Halogen lamps prolong this very burn-out by a unique chemical action.

29 On 13 December 1904, Hungarian Sándor Just and Croatian Franjo Hanaman received a Hungarian patent for a tungsten filament lamp. Soon they were marketed by the Hungarian company Tungsram. They also found that the luminosity of bulbs increased by filling it with an inert gas.

30 Guinness Book of World Records hold The Centennial Light bulb (4 W) as the bulb burning almost continuously at a fire station in Livermore, California, since 1901. A 40-watt bulb in Texas is alive since 21 September 1908.

Halogen Lamps

Halogen lamps have conquered the world in only a short time. They are still tungsten filament bulbs but encased inside a much smaller quartz envelope. They are almost 30% brighter light than from conventional lamps – and up to five times longer life.

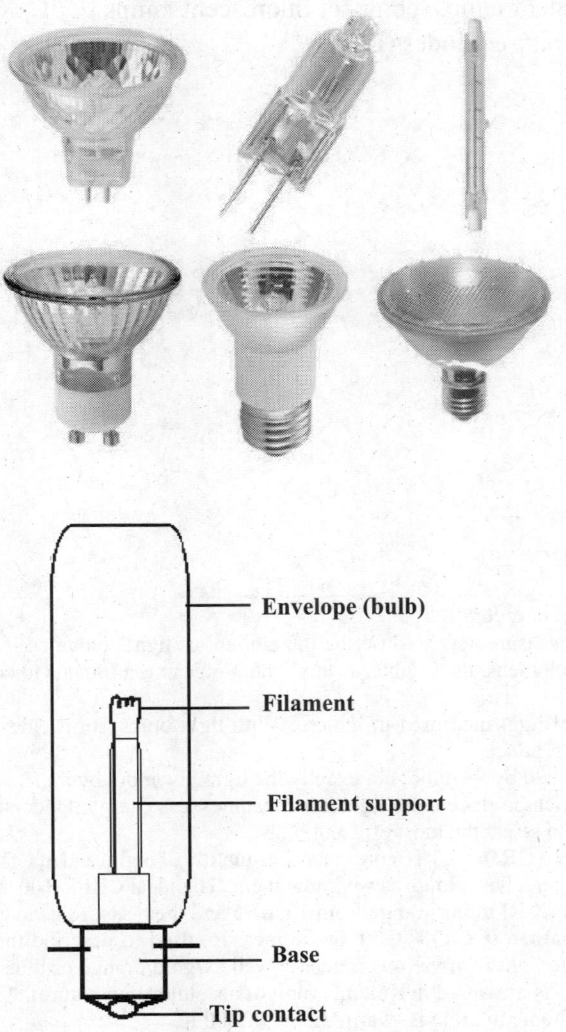

A halogen lamp derives its name from the gases used from the halogen group, such as iodine or bromine. In an ordinary incandescent bulb, tungsten evaporates making the filament weak. But in halogen bulb, it is filled with the halogen gas such as iodine or bromine. At a certain higher temperature, the gas will combine with tungsten atoms as they evaporate and redeposit themselves on the filament, so that the filament material is not effectively lost. So, the filament lasts longer. It has an additional advantage, at higher temperature; you get more light per unit of energy spent. The bulb is extremely hotter than a normal light bulb. At that higher temperature glass would melt. So, it is enclosed in quartz; specially treated quartz (in other words, enriched with UV-absorbent materials) also prevents unwanted ultra violet rays from escaping out of it.

Hence, the halogen bulbs are more brilliant and vibrant, lighting up trade fairs, exhibitions, shops and advertisements. They are taking over as head lamps in automobiles. Being compact and clear they are just right for projectors and such optical systems.

After ruling our nights for a little over 100 years, incandescent light bulbs are giving way to the latest types such as fluorescent lamps, compact fluorescent lamps (CFL), cold cathode fluorescent lamps (CCFL) and light-emitting diodes (LEDs) [31].

31 Small notes on light would be in order;
Lumen - a unit of standard measurement to describe the amount of light contained in an area as perceived by the human eye. The more are the lumens, the brighter is the light. You can use lumens to compare the brightness of any bulb.
Luminous Flux - the flow of light measured in lumens. With light bulbs, it provides an estimate of the apparent amount of light the bulb will produce.
Watts - it is the power consumed by the bulb, not exactly the light given out by it.
We should look for bulbs which produce more light but consumes less energy. Understanding lumens as a measure of brightness makes it easier to select the most efficient bulb.
Colouring Rendering Index (CRI) - CRI represents the quality of light and its faithfulness to render colours correctly, i.e. to enable us to perceive colours as we know them. The ideal CRI is 100, and some incandescent bulbs approach this level. LED bulbs CRI ratings range from 70 to 95 and the best CFLs have ratings in the mid 80s.
Correlated Colour Temperature (CCT) – CCT is the measure used to describe the relative colour appearance of a white light source. White light is in various shades of yellow/gold/orange or blue. Blue light is cool and more yellowish light is warm. CCT is measured in Kelvin's (unit of absolute temperature). 2700 K is 'Warm' and 5000 K is 'Cool.' The typical indoor home lighting is 'warm', 2700 - 2800 K.

Tube Lights

It's a common joke among ourselves, if any one does not understand a thing or two we would call him a tube light. It is also common to picture a bright idea with an incandescent bulb. An incandescent bulb lights up at the flick of a switch but a tube light flickers a few times and then starts. But then a tube light is much more brilliant, saves power, does not throw harsh shadows, but expensive.

Unlike an incandescent lamp the working of tube light is a bit complicated. The tube itself is filled with an inert gas which is non- conducting. It is a little too long for the electric voltage to conduct. Then the tube is coated with white powder which would prevent ordinary light to pass through. But still when you switch it on, quite a few interesting things happen inside the tube light while it flickers a few times and starts.

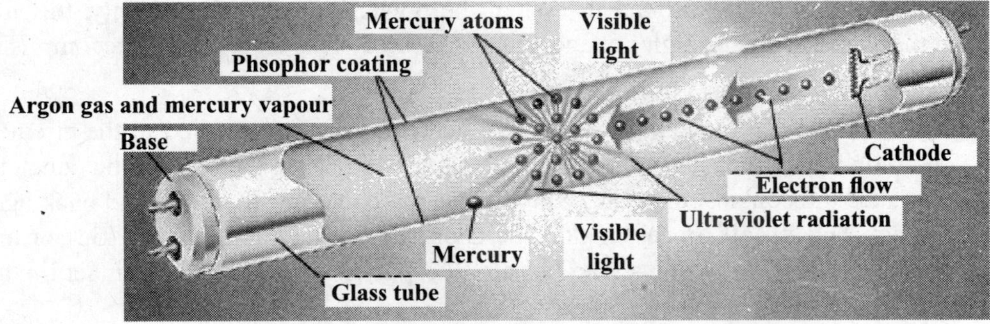

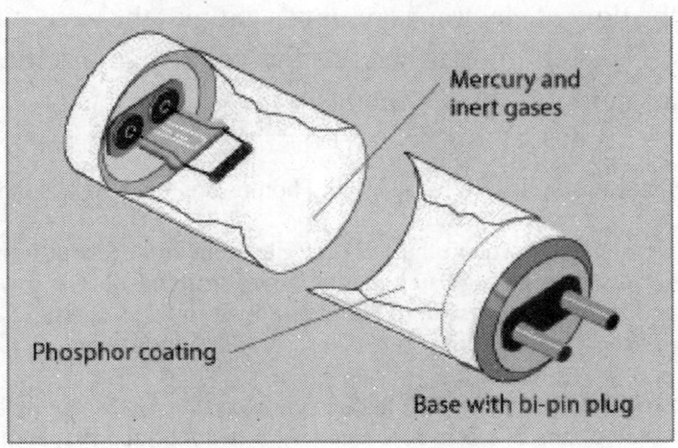

As soon as you switch it on, you can see a red glow on the ends. Those are two heaters on both sides, which heat up the little bit of mercury and turn into gas. This in turn ionizes the gas inside. In other words, the gas becomes conducting. But still it is too long way for the electricity to strike a path. Here comes the starter which along with the choke gives a high voltage kick just enough to strike the path. Tube flickers and then the lighting continues.

But that's not as simple as that. The whole process takes place because of a very fascinating scientific principle[32]. Think of it and then call the tube light a dumb head[33]!

As you turn the lamp on, the electrons will move through the gas from one end to the other. They collide with the gaseous mercury atoms and excite them. In the process, the electrons are bumped into higher energy levels. But as that's an unstable level, they tend to return to their original state. When they do so, they release photons; that's the light. Unfortunately, this light is in the ultraviolet range, in the order of 253 nanometers (nm) wavelength, which is invisible to human eye. Phosphor coating inside the tube converts it into visible light in a process called fluorescence. These lights are known as gas-discharge lamps; tube lights, compact florescent lamps (CFLs), neon lamps, mercury vapour lamps belong to this type.

Parts of a Tube Light:

Choke: It is a small box like unit where a lot of copper wire is wound over an iron core. It gives a very high voltage initially to strike a moving path for the electrons. When the power is switched on, heaters on both ends heat up the mercury, to create a conducting path for the electrons, but it is too long for them to travel. We need a high voltage to make them conducting to the other end. You will generally find that tube light flickers a few times and starts. When power is switched on to a choke, an electromagnetic field is created around it. When the power is taken off suddenly, this field collapses and in the process, a very high voltage spike is created. This on and off is accomplished with the help of a starter.

Starter: It is a neon lamp with bimetallic contacts. When power is first applied to the circuit, it lights up the neon bulb which also heats the gas in the starter and cause the bi-metallic contact to bend away. This makes the contacts to break, which cools the contacts. So, they bend back again and make the contact. This on-off process makes the choke to give out an inductive kick or high voltage spike which starts the lamp. The starter has also a capacitor to prolong the contact life and reduce radio frequency interference.

Once the tube is struck, the flow of electrons continues without the necessity of heating the cathodes or further high voltages. The starter keeps shut as the voltage across the lit tube is insufficient to start a glow, but continues until tube is continuously lit.

32 If you care for a little science;
Light is a form of energy that can be released by an atom. Photons are the most basic units of light. They are released as a result of moving electrons.
In an atom, electrons move in orbitals around the nucleus. Electrons in different orbitals have different amounts of energy. Generally speaking, electrons with greater energy move in orbitals farther away from the nucleus.
When an electron jumps up from a lower orbital to a higher orbital, it takes energy. Conversely, an electron releases energy when it jumps down from a higher orbital to a lower one. That extra energy is released in the form of a photon.

33 Nikola Tesla made some experiments, Edison left them midway. In 1895 one of his former employees, Daniel McFarlan Moore demonstrated lamps 2 to 3 meters (6.6 to 9.8 ft) long tube that emitted pink light. George Inman and Richard Thayer created first commercially viable fluorescent lamp. Mercury-vapour lamp was invented by Peter Cooper Hewitt.

Tube: As the name suggests, tube light is a sealed glass tube with two terminals on each end. The tube contains low pressure Argon gas, or xenon, neon, or krypton. Inside of the tube is coated with fluorescent phosphor powder. The tube also contains a little mercury. There is a heater on each side typically made of coiled tungsten. They are also called cathodes which are connected to the two terminals. The electrical circuit is connected to these terminals.

Advantages[34] **:** Tube lights are more efficient. Typical fluorescent lamp is about 22% efficient in converting input power into visible light compared to 2% of incandescent lamps. Light is more diffused and uniform which does not cast harsh shadows. So, they produce less heat.

Similarly, the life of a tube light is about 10 to 20 times more than an incandescent lamp, though they are costlier and parts are also costlier.

Disadvantages: Tube lights emit small amount of ultraviolet light, which can be detrimental to some paintings and plastics. Tube lights contain small amounts of mercury which is not good for health. Broken fluorescent lamp is hazardous. Flickering tube light is an eyesore. Tube lights also cannot be easily dimmed.

Modern Tube Lights: CFLs are mini tube lights. They fit into existing light bulb holders. Compact fluorescent lamps are small-diameter tube lights where the tube is spiralled to provide a high amount of light output in little volume. CFLs are available in a variety of shapes with two, four, or six tubes. They are almost throwing out good old Edison's light bulb into museums.

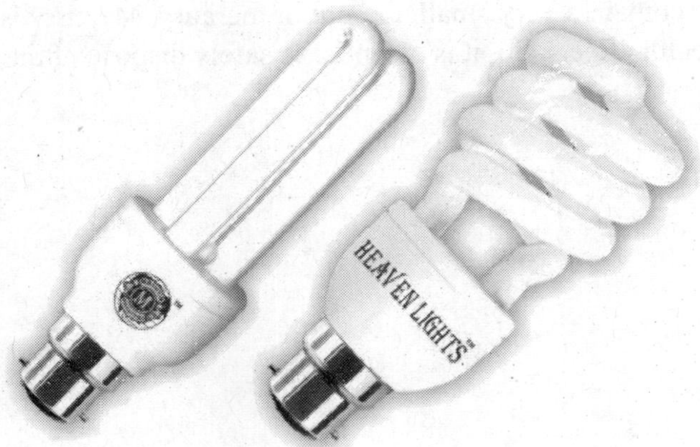

It is long well-known that high frequencies can easily light up the florescent lamps. Modern electronics brought this home and really helped a lot in improving the efficiencies and reduce the flicker. The supply frequency of 50Hz (fifty cycles per second) of domestic AC is converted into high-frequency AC of about 20 kHz. Almost all present CFLs use electronic circuitry, which give them flicker free instant start with increased efficiency.

34 Radio frequency energy can light up a tube light. Place a tube light half way up a two-way radio antenna while it is transmitting. It will light up without any connections.

Other Types of Fluorescent Lamps: There are some other interesting types of fluorescent lamps;

Cold-cathode fluorescent lamps (CCFL): Cold-cathode fluorescent lamps are used as backlighting for LCD displays in personal computers mobile phones and TV monitors.

Germicidal lamps: They use UV light to attract insects which are killed by the high voltage meshing in front of it. They do not contain any phosphor at all. Do not look into the light directly as it can cause eye and skin damage.

Tanning lamps: The lamps are UV lamps used to improve human skin tanning.

Grow lamps: Grow lamps emit light in the red and blue colour range, to aid photosynthesis.

Care and Tips

- ✓ Over years, the ends of tube lights get blackened which indicate its end of life. Discard this and buy a new one.
- ✓ At low voltages, tube light continues to flicker. Nothing can be done for this except wait for the voltage to improve. Modern electronic chokes and CFLs solved this problem of course as they can light up at lower voltages.
- ✓ Bad starter and a bad choke also can show the same flickering. Change one after the other and then the tube itself in that order.
- ✓ Heat reduces the life span of CFL bulbs so also frequent switching on and off. They last longer if they are left for steady periods without switched on and off.
- ✓ Tube lights and CFLs contain a very small amount of mercury. Mercury is a toxic metal which can lead to adverse health effects. So, it is essential to safely dispose of the CFLs and be careful when they break.

Light Emitting Diodes

From being just indicator lamps on transistors or instruments, they formed numbers in the digital displays. Now, they are invading hundred year old Edison's domain of his incandescent lamps and are edging them out. They are the Light Emitting Diodes, commonly called LEDs. They now transmit information from remote controls, light up the so-called LED TVs and give our traffic signals and are ready to light up our homes.

They don't have a filament to burn out, and they don't get hot to touch. They would last at least 10 times longer than CFLs and hundred times more than ordinary light bulbs. They are environment friendly as they do not have any mercury. LED light bulbs use only 1/3rd to 1/30th the power of incandescent bulb or CFL. Though LEDs are initially more costly, they soon pay out and they prices are also continuously falling. In short, Light emitting diode (LED)) bulbs have revolutionized lighting. But the lighting from LEDs is highly directional, unlike incandescent bulbs which spread the light more evenly around an area. However, new design of the fixtures solve this problem to a large extent.

Light Output: Do you know that a standard 60 W incandescent bulb gives about 300-900 lumens of light. CFL takes about 13 to 18 watts to give out the same amount of light, whereas LED will take only 4 to 5 watts. Here is a comparative chart.

Light Output	**LEDs**	**CFLs**	**Incandescents**
Lumens	*Watts*	*Watts*	*Watts*
450	4 - 5	8 - 12	40
300 - 900	6 - 8	13 - 18	60
1100 - 1300	9 - 13	18 - 22	75 - 100
1600 - 1800	16 - 20	23 - 30	100
2600 - 2800	25 - 28	30 - 55	150

Let There be Light: Light is a form of energy that can be released by an atom. Photons are the most basic units of light. A 'Light Emitting Diode' or LED is a specialised junction diode. Diode is an electronic component which allows flow of current only in one direction. In LEDs, positive anode and negative cathode junction is created by special semi conductor materials like gallium arsenide which are suitably doped. Electrons emitted by electrodes are drawn to the p-n junction. Electrons jump to the side of the junction where there is a depletion of electrons, otherwise known as holes. In this condition when electrons are falling into lower energy levels, photons are released. When gallium arsenide is used as semiconductor material, we get red LED.

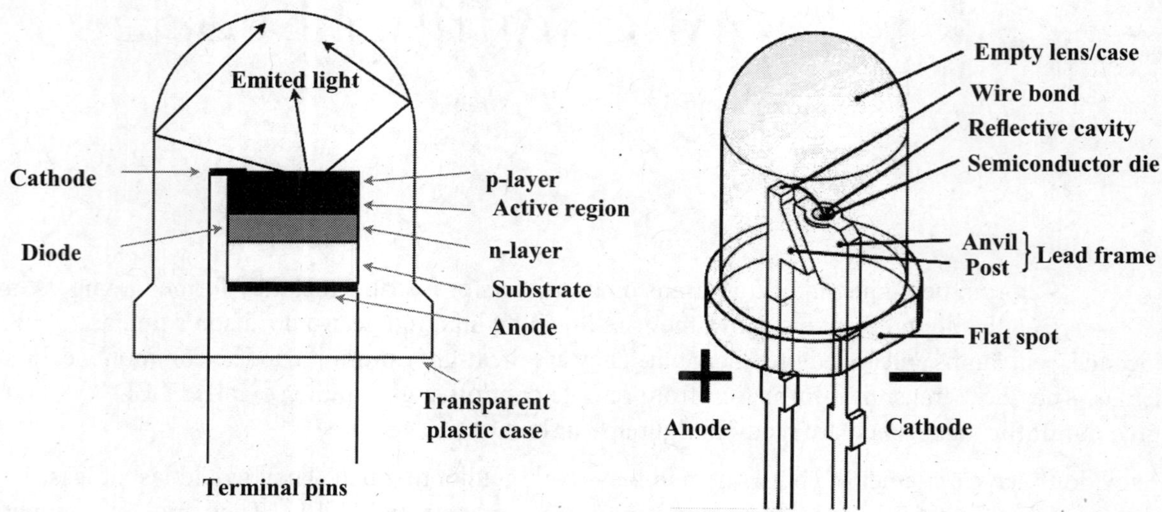

The color of an LED is determined by the semiconductor material, not by the coloring of the plastic body. The plastic body is often colored to diffuse and enhance the light output and also to indicate its colour when it is not illuminated. LEDS are also available in clear packages. LEDs are available in a wide range of colours like red, blue, amber, yellow, green and of course blue and white.

They are also available in infra red as well as in multi-coloured range. Here is a table showing the compound materials, wave length and colour emitted, and minimum forward voltage required.

Color and Current: All LEDS need a minimum voltage and a minimum current to operate properly[35]. LEDs work typically at low voltages of about 1.2 for an infra red LED to about 4 volts for white LED. They draw currents between about 10 and 40 mill amperes. Voltages and currents above these values can straight away kill an LED. LEDs cannot work the other way round for they work only when they are forward biased, which means that they are properly connected.

Typical LED Characteristics

Semiconductor Material	Wavelength	Colour	VF @ 20mA
GaAs	850-940 nm	Infra-Red	1.2 v
GaAsP	630-660 nm	Red	1.8 v
GaAsP	605-620 nm	Amber	2.0 v
GaAsP:N	585-595 nm	Yellow	2.2 v
AlGaP	550-570 nm	Green	3.5 v

35 Oleg Vladimirovich Losev of Russia created the first LED in 1927, but it was forgotten until 1962 when Nick Holonyak, Jr., developed a red LED while working at General Electric Company.

Semiconductor Material	Wavelength	Colour	VF @ 20mA
SiC	430-505 nm	Blue	3.6 v
GaInN	450 nm	White	4.0 v

There are two wires below an LED, one is shorter and one is longer. The LED has a flat side on the body; the shorter wire also comes on this side. This wire is connected to the negative terminal of a battery. So, never connect an LED directly to a battery or power supply! It will see the end of the day almost instantly because very high current passing through it. So, LEDs must have a resistor in series to limit the current to a safe value.

World is craving for energy efficient lighting systems as lighting takes more than 25% of the average home electricity bills. LED lighting will reduce that bill but presently they are expensive. They also have more focussed light rather than diffused and uniform lighting like CFLs. Also colour rendering index (CRI) of LEDs is low. LEDs also have limited temperature tolerance which limits their usable power or their number in a given fitting. Above all they have an extremely long life which poses a problem for bulb manufacturers, who thrive on replacements.

They are good number of projects to work with LEDs. If you are a project man, look into some in my book 'Exciting Electronic Experiments' from Pustak Mahal.

Telephone

Those of you who are accustomed to push button, cordless or mobile phones, you missed a lot about those good old telephones.

- The original phones were cranky; yes they had to be cranked to generate a voltage and make a call.
- To talk to someone outside your village or town, you had to book a call at the local post office and wait for hours to days for the call to materialize.
- When it comes on, you really had to talk at the top of your voice.
- But then whole system as it is, it stood the test of time. If you have an antique phone from the 1920s[36], you could still connect it and it would work just fine!
- But after standing tall for over 100 years, it is just on its way out, just like an incandescent bulb.

Telephone is one of the most amazing devices ever created. Just press a few buttons or dial a number, you are instantly connected to that person and both of you can talk to each other anywhere in the world.

Since its early years, the telephone instrument is comprised of a few practical parts; a power source, a switch hook, a dialler, a ringer, a transmitter, a receiver, and an anti-side tone circuit.

36 When a telephone was first displayed at the Centennial Exhibition in Philadelphia in 1876, Brazilian Emperor Dom Pedro exclaimed, 'My God, it talks!'

Hook switch: Cradle switch to connect and disconnect the phone from the network. As soon as you lift the phone, the switch inside connects you to the local telephone exchange which supplies it with the direct current through the local loop. It also connects you to the low-frequency 'dial tone' —actually two simultaneous tones of 350 and 440 hertz. When the telephone is 'on hook,' contact with the local loop is broken but telephone would be ready to receive a call.

Receiver: The receiver is the small little speaker in the earpiece of the telephone's handset. It operates on Faraday's electromagnetic laws. A diaphragm fixed to coils of insulated fine wire. The coil of wire is centrally placed in a permanent magnet. It converts fluctuating electric current into sound waves that reproduce human speech. Telephone receivers have limited response in the audio frequencies of 350 to 3,500 hertz, sufficient to reproduce normal speech.

Transmitter: A microphone transmits our speech into telephone lines. In the past, telephones used to have carbon microphones with carbon granules compressed between two thin metal plates. These granules are compressed or decompressed due to the sound waves from your voice. This changes their resistance which in effect modulates the current flowing through the microphone. But presently almost all the telephones have electrets microphones which are tiny, yet very sensitive[37]. Due to their high performance and low cost, these microphones virtually replaced all other types from telephone transmitters to high-fidelity recording microphones.

Dialer: The dialer is used to call the number of the party that we wish to talk to. The traditional rotary dialler, invented in the 1890s is still in vogue at many places but they are vastly replaced by the push button type. When this dialler is turned with a finger and released, it makes a number of make and break contacts. They make interruptions or pulses of approximately one-tenth of a second in the flow of direct current to the telephone exchange. This operates a number of relays and connects this line to the numbered line. This is what is known as pulse dialling.

Push button dialling still gives a scope for pulse dialling; it is slowly being replaced by tone dialling which was introduced in the 1960s. Each press of a button generates a 'dual-tone' signal that is specific to button, in turn to its number. Each dual tone is composed of a low frequency and a high frequency tone, which designate the number dialled. Compared to rotary diallers, they are faster and can activate automated functions at the other end of the line.

All telephone switches still recognize 'pulse dialling.'

Ringer: 'When the telephone rings', 'Give me a ring' are some of the commonly used sentences referring to the telephone alerts. The original ringers were mechanical, never changed until a few decades ago, when electronic ringers came up. Both types are activated alternating pulses (two-second on and four seconds off) generated by the telephone exchange. These pulses activate bell which gives that classical telephone ring.

In modern electronic ringers, electronic circuits generate the tones which are heard through a tiny loud speaker.

Anti-sidetone circuit: This is an interesting part of the telephone. The anti-sidetone circuit prevents you from hearing your own voice. Have you thought that there is something like it inside and think

37 An electret microphone is a condenser microphone invented by Gerhard Sessler and Jim West at Bell laboratories in 1962.

of the cacophony without it. A device called a duplex coil or its equivalent blocks the sound of your own voice from reaching your ear.

Power source: Telephone works on the standard voltage is 48 volts with a ringing voltage of 75 volts which is supplied through a two-wire circuit called the local loop.

Calling Someone[38]: While the hundred year old operation was mostly mechanical activated by electrical relays, the telephone system remain unchanged except that now electronics play the major part. When you take the telephone off its cradle and dial a number, a combination of tones pass through the two wires from your homes to the local exchange. It generates a ringing tone at the called phone if it is on-hook. If it is off hook, it means that the phone is engaged or someone is using that phone. Then the exchange generates engage tone back to your phone. As soon as the other party lifts the phone, ringing tone is cut off by the exchange and both the phones are connected for talking.

Care and Tips

Telephones are basically rugged devices. Most often the network problems, wiring in and from the house and in the exchange create problems. With the globalisation, telephone repairs are faster, but once the telephone mechanic was the most sought after persons.

But here are tips for good telephone conversation.

- ✓ Dial the correct number so as not to disturb strangers.
- ✓ If the number dialled is wrong, simply say, 'Sorry, wrong number.'
- ✓ When the number you are calling is not answered quickly, wait long enough. It is very annoying to pick up the telephone and find the caller has hung up.
- ✓ Make sure that your conversations with people are as brief as possible.
- ✓ When you pick up the telephone, put a smile on your face and announce your name as soon as 'Hello!' is over.
- ✓ Listen attentively and answer.
- ✓ Do not interrupt conversations. Do not allow yourself to be distracted by other activities while speaking on the telephone. Multi-tasking is the enemy of effective listening.
- ✓ Let your caller finish speaking before you talk. Let not words jumble up, which is no good for both of you.
- ✓ Match the speed of your voice with that of the caller.
- ✓ After finishing the talk, do not slam the receiver down, even if you are angry. The caller may still have the phone close to his ear, and then a sudden bang can harm his ear and your conversation.

38

March 10, 1876, Alexander Graham Bell spoke into the phone, 'Mr. Watson, come here. I need you.' Thomas A. Watson sitting in the next room came running and declared that he had heard every word Bell spoke. When Bell asked him to repeat the words, Watson repeated them. Those were the very first words ever to be transmitted by the telephone.

In a 1912 issue of Popular Mechanics, Bell recalled, 'To tell the truth, as a practical man, I did not quite believe it; as a theoretical man, I saw a speaking telephone by which we could have the means of transmitting speech and reproducing it in distant places.'

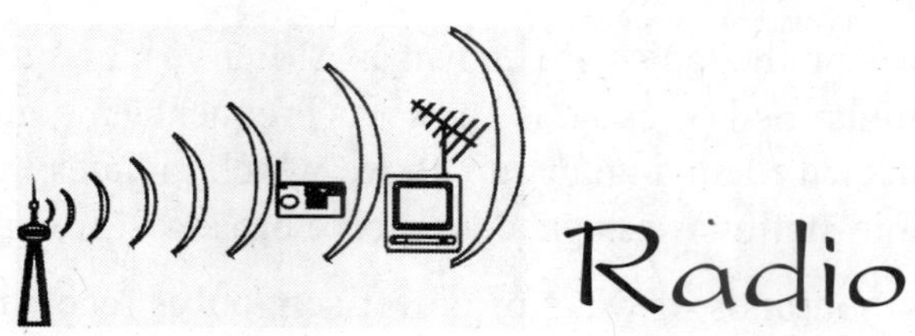

Radio

We are surrounded! Someone is talking on his cell phone through our body. Some radio station is transmitting its program across our body; pictures transmitted by another TV station are passing through us. 'Radio waves' - invisible and utterly undetectable to humans, they have totally transformed the modern society. Whether it is a cell phone, or a cordless phone or AM and FM radio, Radio-controlled toy, Television, GPS receiver, Ham radio, wireless Internet access, or radar, all of them use radio waves. From microwave oven to an airplane to artificial satellite all depend on radio waves. The interesting aspect behind all this, radio is an incredibly simple technology, just over 100 years[39].

We will talk about the simple radio now which we use to listen to the news, music or talks[40]. Any radio set-up has two parts: the transmitter and the receiver. Let us first transmit and then listen.

Waves Audible and Inaudible: When we talk into a microphone, it converts our voice sound waves into electromagnetic waves in the frequency range of 20-20,000 cycles per second. What is this frequency? It is the number of times the voice waves oscillate up and down per second. They are known as cycles per second or Hertz (Hz) named after the great scientist. Human ear cannot hear the sound waves beyond this range, the audio frequency range. Unfortunately the electromagnetic waves in this range cannot travel far, even if they are amplified well.

When the frequencies are increased to hundreds of thousand cycles, they can travel far and wide. But they do not contain any intelligence or information. A simple analogy is like this. We have a limp man who cannot walk but can see. We also have a blind man who cannot see but can walk. Solution is simple. Ask the blind man to carry the limp who will show the way. That is exactly what they do in radio transmission. Make the higher frequency carry the lower audio frequency.

Modulation: Let us say, All India Radio, Visakhapatnam is transmitting at 927 kilo cycles per second. Radio station generates a pure wave of 927 KHz. Audio from the record or talk is made to ride over it and now it can travel far and wide. In other words, the audio modulates or encodes the high frequency wave. The high frequency wave is aptly called the carrier wave and the process is known as modulation. In this mode, the amplitude of the carrier wave is changed, so it is known as

39 In 1895, Alexander Stepanovich Popov built his first radio receiver. According to the proceedings of the United States Naval Institute in 1899, the Marconi instruments had a '[...] coherer, principle of which was discovered some twenty years ago, [and was] the only electrical instrument or device contained in the apparatus that is at all new.'

40 On June 3, 1900, Brazilian priest Roberto Landell de Moura transmitted the human voice by wireless in Brazil for a distance of approximately 8 km.

amplitude modulation (AM) and the radios are known as AM radios. Frequency of the carrier wave also can be changed in a similar method and it is known as Frequency modulation (FM). These high frequency signals are connected to an antenna up above which radiates them into the air and the vacuum of space. Every radio station is assigned a specific broadcast frequency.

Now a tiny fraction of the thousands of watts of power sent out is received by the antenna in the radio at home. That's about a few milli or microwatts of the transmitted signal. But then we have lakhs or millions of radio stations all around, broadcasting in different frequencies. So, a tuner in the radio selects the station we want and that signal is amplified. Then the signal is demodulated and voice frequencies are separated. Audio is now amplified and a speaker delivers the sound waves.

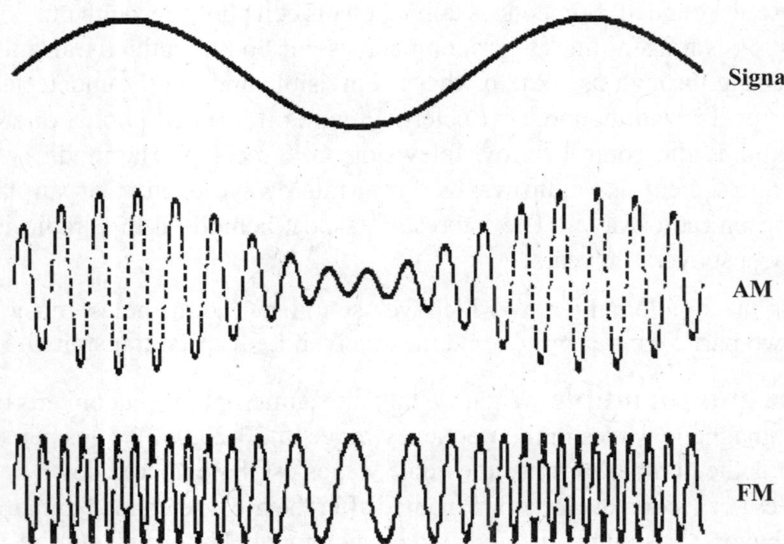

Sounds simple and some ingenious circuits make this possible. Almost all the devices, whether it is a radio, cell phone, cordless phone, or television and a host of others work on the same principle!

There are three methods of modulation – pulse modulation, amplitude modulation and frequency modulation. In pulse modulation, the carrier wave is turned on or off depending on the information signal like in the Morse code. In amplitude modulation, the amplitude of the carrier wave is changed. AM radio and the picture part of a TV signal are encoded by AM. In frequency modulation, the frequency of the carrier wave is changed based on the information signal. FM transmission is largely immune to static unlike AM. FM radios, the sound portion of a TV signal, cordless phones, cell phones, etc., use frequency modulation.

Let us have a peep into the radio now.

Antenna: Both the transmitter and receiver use antennas to radiate and capture the radio signal. You must have observed a little telescopic rod sticking out of old transistor radios or the Yagi antenna on the roof top for the television reception. Modern cell phones have much smaller antennae, as they use much higher frequency. It can be anything from a long, stiff wire to a satellite dish. The size and shape are designed to the frequency of the radio signal.

Tuner: The antenna receives all the thousands of radio waves. The tuner selects the station you want to receive. The tuners resonate at one particular frequency, capture and amplify it. Now this signal is filtered and brought down to a common frequency known as an Intermediate frequency to achieve a uniformly good amplification.

Detector or Demodulator: Now, the intermediate frequency is still a composite signal from which the audio signal needs to be separated. In AM radios, the detector is a simple electronic device called a diode. In FM, it is carried out by a little more complicated method.

Audio Amplifier: The detected audio signal is very weak. Audio amplifier amplifies the milliwatt audio signal to stronger signal to be audible by human ear.

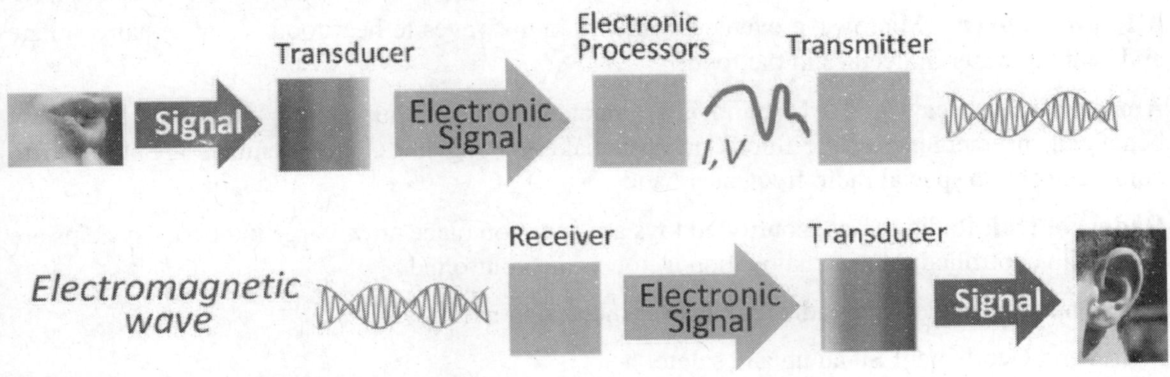

Speaker: A speaker converts electrical energy into mechanical energy, in other words, the electromagnetic waves are converted to sound waves. A microphone does the reverse; it converts sound waves into electromagnetic waves.

Circuit Board: The circuit board contains all the components for the antenna, tuner, and switches for changing bands and on-off, frequency conversion, demodulation, amplifiers, and speaker. Often all of them are mounted on a single printed circuit board. Early radios had valves or vacuum tubes as the active components and the radios filled a table top. With the introduction of transistors [41], the sizes have shrunk to tiny sizes. Power consumption also reduced and they can be used with small batteries. Advent of integrated circuits further reduced their sizes.

Ionosphere helps in AM transmission. So, AM can reach far and wide and can even go round the world in certain conditions. But AM is noisy as it can pick up various electromagnetic disturbances. FM does not pick up static noises and interferences. Its audio frequency range is also higher compared to AM and its quality is also greater. It is transmitted in the very high frequency (VHF, 30 MHz to 300 MHz) radio spectrum. But it travels in straight lines and hence the reception range is generally limited to about 100 kilometers.

Normal TV sound is FM but the picture is transmitted in AM. Most new radio systems are digital.

41 In 1954, Regency company introduced a pocket transistor radio, powered by a 'standard 22.5 V Battery.' In 1955, Sony company introduced its first transistorized radio, small enough to fit in a Pocket, powered by a small battery

Other Radio Systems: Radio communication so far was one way, i.e. a single transmitter sends signals to many receivers. There are 'simplex' systems where two persons talk one after the other or one at a time, say walky- talkies. But in cordless or cell phones, two persons continuously and concurrently talk. It is called 'duplex' operation.

To increase the number of persons sharing the same frequency, particularly in cell phones, interesting techniques known as frequency-division multiplexing (FDM), time-division multiplexing (TDM) and code-division multiplexing (CDM) are used.

Radar: Radar (Radio Detection and Ranging) is used to detect ships or airplanes. Radio waves are sent and reflections are received. The objects can be precisely positioned.

VOR: VOR (Very high frequency omni-directional range) systems are used by aircraft for instrument landing.

Microwave ovens: Microwave ovens use intense radio waves to heat food. They actually agitate and heat the water molecules in the food.

Amateur radio service: HAM radio is an amateur hobby radio system, which has been very beneficial in emergencies like floods or earthquakes saving lives. The members are licensed to communicate on special radio frequency band.

Radio control: Radio remote controlled toys are common place now. Large industrial systems are now radio controlled. Marine navigation is now radio controlled.

So, we have surrendered to radio and its ever increasing uses.

Ladies and Gentlemen! Stand up and salute!

Nikloa Tesla[42] and Jagadish Chandra Bose[43] !

42 In 1893, Serbian-American inventor, Nikola Tesla made radio devices for his experiments and predicted a cell phone.

43 In November 1894, public demonstration at Town Hall of Kolkata, Jagadish Chandra Bose ignited gunpowder and rang a bell at a distance using millimetre range wavelength microwaves. Bose wrote in a Bengali essay, Adrisya Alok (Invisible Light), 'The invisible light can easily pass through brick walls, buildings etc. Therefore, messages can be transmitted by means of it without the mediation of wires.' He submitted his scientific papers to the Asiatic Society of Bengal in May 1895 and the Royal Society of London in October 1895. In December 1895, the London journal the Electrician (Vol. 36) published Bose's paper, 'On a new electro-polariscope'. At that time, the word 'coherer', coined by Lodge, was used in receivers or detectors. The Englishman (18 January 1896) commented as follows:'Should Professor Bose succeed in perfecting and patenting his 'Coherer', we may in time see the whole system of coast lighting throughout the navigable world revolutionised by a Bengali scientist working single handed in our Presidency College Laboratory.' Bose planned to 'perfect his coherer' but never thought of patenting it.

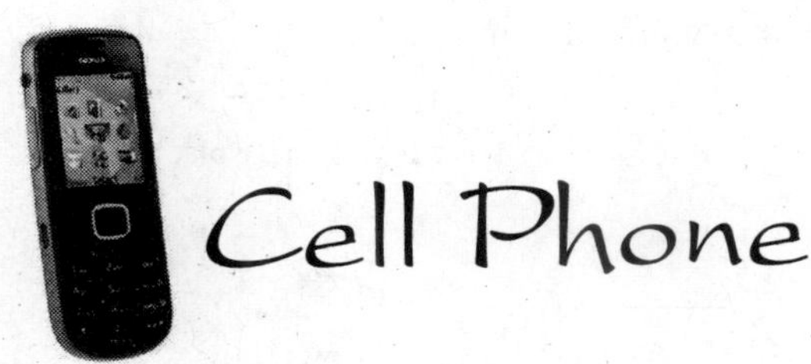

Cell Phone

After the advent of cell phones, the world has become flat and shrunk. Cell phones are some of the most complicated devices that we play with. The technology is mind boggling as these phones receive, transmit and process millions of mathematical calculations per second.

The truth remains that it is a complex radio, albeit a radio. But for a small little gadget weighing about 100 gms [44], they are loaded with a host of unheard of services. Call it a mobile phone or cellular phone, cell phone or a hand phone, or smart phone! Apart from all those so-called 'Apps', its main function is to make and receive telephone calls while moving around a wide geographic area, well, over a radio link. That is where the complexity begins! Modern mobile phones support a whole range of other facilities such as SMS [45], MMS, email, Internet access, infrared; Bluetooth, banking, business, calculators, games, photography and videography and new ones are continuously added. On the other hand, a cordless phone is used only within the short range, single, and private.

In the early 1950s', cell phones were developed for use in automobiles; thus the name mobile phone. It was like driving around the city with an entire telephone company in the car boot.

Cells, Hexagonal Cells: To solve this problem each geographical area was divided into small cells usually in the shape of hexagons. Now, each of these cells has its own base station and transmitting and receiving tower and antennae. The cell phones have low-power transmitters (either 0.3 watts or 6 watts) and very sensitive receivers. That makes the radio link. These towers are in link with the cell phones in their area of operation, whether you are making a call or not. It is a kind of a handshake signal with a designated system identification code (SID). As soon the cell phone is switched on a handshake, with SID is established between the tower and the phone. The tower knows that you are here. But if this link is not established 'NO SERVICE' message is displayed. Once the link is available, you can send a call or receive. In the process, service provider also sends a registration code whereby the customer can be located.

44 The first hand-held mobile phone was weighed about 1 kg, appropriately nicknamed 'the brick'. Recalling the first call he made on that mobile phone on 3 April 1973. Dr Martin Cooper of Motorola said, 'As I walked down the street while talking on the phone, sophisticated New Yorkers gaped at the sight of someone actually moving around while making a phone call. Remember that in 1973, there weren't cordless telephones or cellular phones. I made numerous calls, including one where I crossed the street while talking to a New York radio reporter - probably one of the more dangerous things I have ever done in my life.'
The new invention costed about $3,995.

45 The first SMS text message was sent from a computer to a mobile phone in 1992 in the UK, while the first person-to-person SMS from phone to phone was sent in Finland in 1993.

But what happens when one moves from cell to cell?

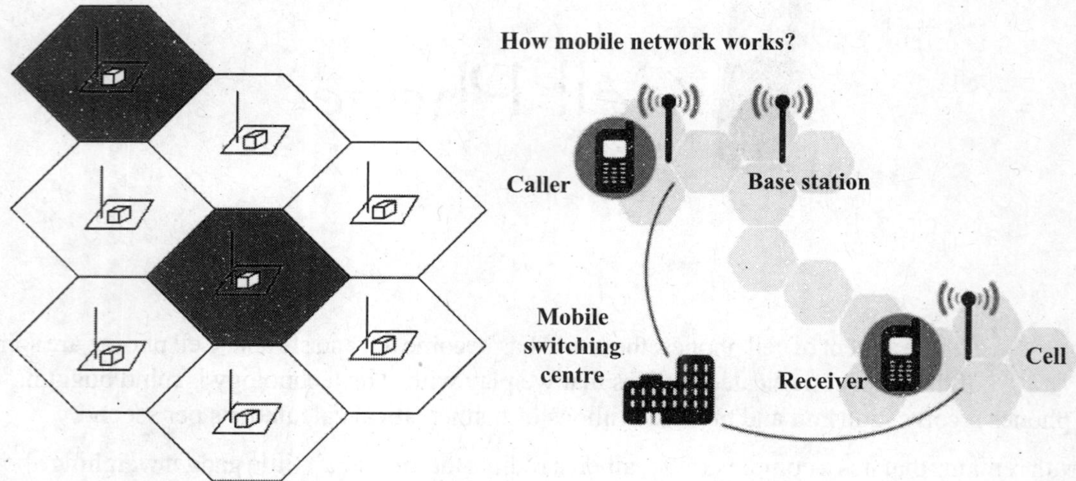

Let us say that you are riding a car. The signal to the present tower is weakening but in the meanwhile signal is getting stronger at another tower. When the towers sense this, they switch the call to a different frequency in just milliseconds. And you do not know but you keep talking! This is called a hand-off in the cell phone technology.

Technology In Your Palm: Amazing technology that fits into your palm! When you take it apart there are only few interesting parts. There is the microphone, the speaker, the battery and the antenna of course.

Speaker would be the size of a rupee coin and the microphone the size of small Bindi. Ever wonder how well most of them reproduce sound! Most of the present day batteries are lithium ion types which give maximum power to the size compared to all other batteries.

The circuit board is the brain of the system. It has a microprocessor which control, command and processes all the functions of the phone. It interacts and enables the key pad or touch screen and displays the information. Signalling to and fro the base station, other functions of the cell are all processed by this chip. There are memory chips like ROM and flash memory on the board to support operating systems. RF section deals with FM radio frequency in and out. Power section takes care of the power management.

In the simple language our speech is in analogue mode while the entire operations of the cell phone are in the digital mode. So there are analogue-to-digital and digital-to-analogue convertor chips which convert them into suitable formats. Then, there is a Digital signal processor (DSP) which manipulates the signals at a real high speed.

A liquid crystal display (LCD) - We have come a long way in displays; there are high resolution and multicolour. One of the greatest advantages of a cell phone is that we can know who is on the line, take it or leave it.

A keyboard is the input device. Looks like the typical key board is on its way out with the displays doubling up as touch inputs! The most common touch systems are the resistance, the capacitive and the surface acoustic wave system. The resistive system is the cheapest; its quality is the lowest of the three, and the surface acoustic wave set-up is usually the most expensive.

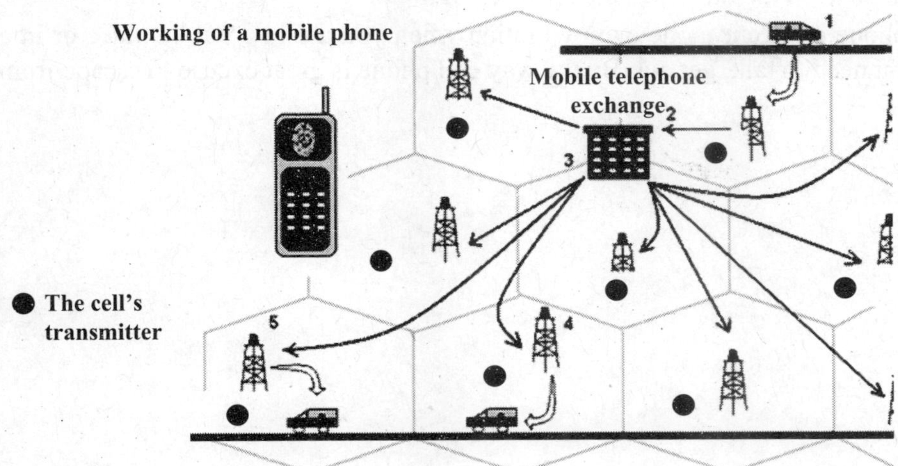

Then there is the cell phone tower which gives its foot print or its range and also receives and transmits the signals. It is a tall steel pole that rises hundreds of feet into the air. Right on top is the antenna and at the base of the tower is the processing equipment. Often a number of service providers share a common pole.

Another interesting part of a GSM cell phone is the subscriber identity module or SIM card. It is a small microchip approximately the size of a small postage stamp. SIM card can be changed from one phone to the other to get access to that phone. We now have phones that accommodate two or three SIM cards.[46]

While I do not wish to discuss on the features and facilities of the cell phones, which everyone knows well, there are certain sidelights[47], I would prefer to stress. Remember, cell phones are our friends, not our masters. They don't control us or they shouldn't at least. I have been seeing a generation clinging to them desperately.

Please note that the service provider can track the movements of a mobile phone user, his SIM card and the handset.

Of late there is raging debate and an intense study on the effect cell phone radiation on human health. While there are pros and cons, on 31st May 2011, the World Health Organization declared that its use may pose a long-term health risk.

46 The first SIM card was made in 1991 by Munich smart card maker Giesecke & Devrient for the Finnish wireless network operator Radiolinja.

47 The world's first commercial automated cellular network was launched in Japan by NTT in 1979. The phone had a talk time of just half an hour and took ten hours to charge.
In 1991, the second generation (2G) cellular technology was launched in Finland by Radiolinja. Ten years later, in 2001, the third generation (3G) was launched in Japan by NTT DoCoMo.

It's good to follow a few rules of etiquette when you are using a cell phone.

- ✓ All those rules of a normal phone apply unequivocally. But then with a cell phone you are always not at home, so keep the other person's privacy in mind.
- ✓ Try to keep your phone on silent mode or in vibration when you are in a public place or in a meeting. Should you need to talk, get out. By the way cell phone is great excuse to escape from a boring lecture.

Television

The story of television reads like a thriller [48]. After man succeeded in transmitting and receiving voice wirelessly, his quest started to transmit image over the air. But God himself has created provisions in the human brain to achieve this.

The First Principle: If you divide an image into a collection of small colored dots, your brain will reassemble the dots into a meaningful image. This is no small feat; you will agree after the end of this article. TV or computer screen contains thousands of these dots called pixels. Even if you blow up a newspaper image to a larger size, you will find thousands of these dots.

The human brain's next amazing feature: If you divide a moving scene into a series of still pictures and show the still images in rapid succession, the brain will view the still images as a moving scene. This is called persistence of vision. Movie pictures are projected by individual frames all at once optically at a speed of 22 frames per second and you will not notice the flicker. However to transmit electronically, we have to split into a number of dots.

Television and computer monitors use both the principles. So, split the image into number of frames and transmit them in rapid succession. The brain will look at it as a moving picture.

So a scene is scanned, just as we read a book line after line. Just as we turn the page and read on, the moving picture is also transmitted as number of pages or frames in rapid succession. Television at our homes builds the picture similarly, but it is done so fast that you barely notice the flicker. That's what happens in a television whether it uses a cathode ray picture tube (CRT) or Liquid Crystal display (LCD) or plasma.

Sounds simple but incredibly complex electromagnetic waves enter our television set and are processed. Black and white picture is just shades of grey. Colour picture is encoded in degrees of red, green and blue, Add to this a synchronising signal, hide the retrace lines (when we finish a line in a page, we quickly jump to the first word in the next line – that's retrace), make and break

48 John Logie Baird developed the first television calling it 'Televisor.' It was a mechanical contraption made out of an old tea chest, a cardboard disc cut from a hatbox (a homemade Nipkow disc) and lamp in a discarded biscuit box. Baird displayed his television system with a resolution of 30 lines to the members of the Royal Institution on January 26, 1926. But people were sceptical. When Logie Baird took his television machine to the Daily Express, he was promptly sent away. As Baird walked out, the editor called up his aide and told him, 'Go down to reception and get rid of a lunatic who's down there. He says he's got a machine for seeing by wireless! Be careful! He may have a razor on him!'

frames, modulate this entire signal on a high frequency carrier wave so that it can travel in air. And then add modulated sound signal. Transmit as a radio wave for our antenna or cable to pick up. Still sounding simple?

Inside TV: Let us switch on the television with the good old cathode ray tube (CRT). The picture tube on which we see the image is actually a vacuum tube. We see the picture at the wide end, whose inner surface is coated with phosphors. Phosphors are chemical substances that light up when a charged electrical particle hits them. Different kinds of phosphors produce different colours, but a combination of in various intensities of only red, blue, and green can create a good colour picture. The narrow end contains an ion gun, which shoots out a series of charged particles of electricity. Colour picture tube has three guns for red, green and blue. The stream of electrons is focused so that it specifically and correctly targets the right phosphor. The electron stream is accelerated by an accelerating anode. Really very high voltages are required to accomplish the electron travel from end to end. The tube is vaccumised and hence the name of vacuum tube. The 'cathode' is a heated filament (like the filament in a normal light bulb). The 'ray' is a stream of electrons that naturally pour off a heated cathode into the vacuum. So, the name cathode ray tube (CRT). This narrow, high-speed ray of electrons travels in the vacuum hits the flat screen at the other end of the tube.

A series of deflection coils or electromagnets deflect the electron rays precisely to the target points on the inside back of the screen we look at. These are kind of steering coils made up of copper windings. One set moves the electron beam vertically, while another set moves it horizontally. The ray travels from left to right one line at a time across the screen. It then quickiy flies back to the left side, moves down to the next line and writes another horizontal line, and so on. Interestingly all the odd lines scanned first and then the even lines. This is known as interlaced scanning where the entire screen is scanned 25 times every second in two passes. Most computer monitors use progressive scanning because it significantly reduces flicker.

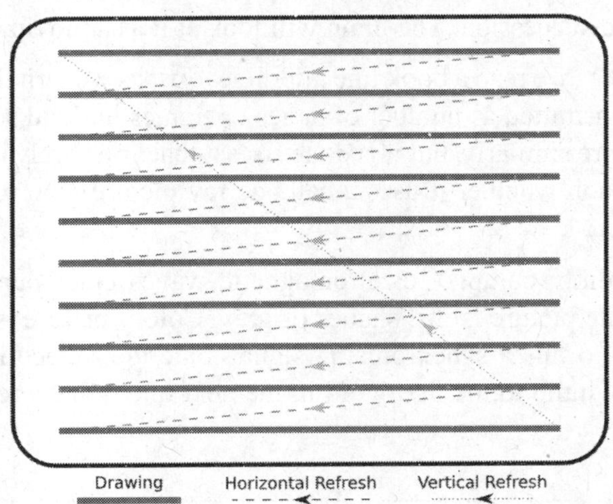

A shadow mask or aperture grill just in front of the screen phosphors directs the red, green or blue signal exactly to the right phosphor and you get a crisp, vibrant image with high contrast ratio and a large viewing angle. But CRTs are quite heavy because they are made up of glass and they also consume a lot of power.

Cathode Ray Tube: With the advent of LCDs and Plasmas, CRT televisions are on their way out but the principles of operation are still the same. In India, the picture is scanned into 625 lines with 50 frames per second and the colour is encoded by PAL system. We have read about

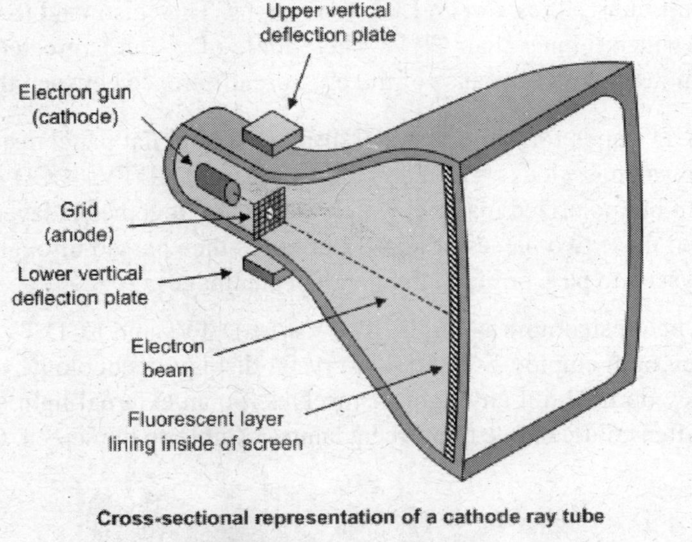

Cross-sectional representation of a cathode ray tube

modulation in the article on radio. In television the composite video signal is amplitude-modulated and the sound is frequency-modulated.

New technologies like LCD or plasma consume much less but they all make use of the same process of reception and picture scanning[49]. Let us have a look at them.

Plasma Screen: Plasma is actually a gas with ions and electrons. Under normal conditions, the gas has a balanced position with equal number of positive charged particles [protons] and negative charged particles [electrons].

If a voltage is applied to the gas, the number of electrons increases and the free electrons knock out lose some more electrons from the atoms. They get a more positive charge and so becomes an ion. Both the electrons and ions get attracted to each other causing inter collision. This collision causes photons of energy are released, which is nothing but light. We see this in florescent light.

A plasma television screen consists of a number of minuscule cells filled with neon and xenon gases separated by two glass panels. Each cell is linked to an electrode. The electrode excites the

49 Originally the scanning was done mechanically until a 14-year-old farm boy, Philo. T. Farnsworth thought of scanning the image electronically when he was tilling a potato field. He spoke about his idea for electronic television to his chemistry teacher, Justin Tolman. The teacher was startled and asked: 'Television? What's that?' Year later the same teacher testified in the court in his students favour in a court battle.
On September 7, 1927, Farnsworth transmitted a thick horizontal line and received it in a picture tube made out of a chemistry flask. Television was born on a chemistry flask! He won a prolonged fight with Radio Corporation of America reads like a thriller, when they wanted to steal his rights legally or illegally.
His comment on television: 'There's nothing on it worthwhile, and we're not going to watch it in this household, and I don't want it in your intellectual diet.'

gases contained in the cell, which emit charged particles. The particles strike red, green, or blue phosphors. The phosphors light up, creating the image seen on the television screen.

Plasma TVs produce pictures with very high contrast. They also have good refresh rates, so that fast moving images don't blur as they can on LCD televisions. They also tend to be thicker than LCD televisions, though much thinner than CRTs. Their angle of vision is greater. Unfortunately they cannot be used in high altitudes, because of the pressure difference between the gas and the air.

LCD Screen: LCD stands for 'liquid-crystal display,' a thin, flat panel display that you can see everywhere now in watches, clocks, calculators to laptops and HDTVs. LCD panels consist of two layers of transparent but polarized material which are 'glued' together. A layer of liquid crystals is sandwiched between these two pieces of glass. Current is then passed through individual crystals, which allow the crystals to pass or block light and create images.

There is a lot of hype created now selling LED TVs. LED TVs and LCD TVs are very similar in construction, as they both employ LCD (liquid-crystal display) technology. LCD screens need to be lighted up as they do not emit any light themselves. So an external light source is required. A backlight — most often cold-cathode fluorescent lamp — lights up the screen. Of late light-emitting

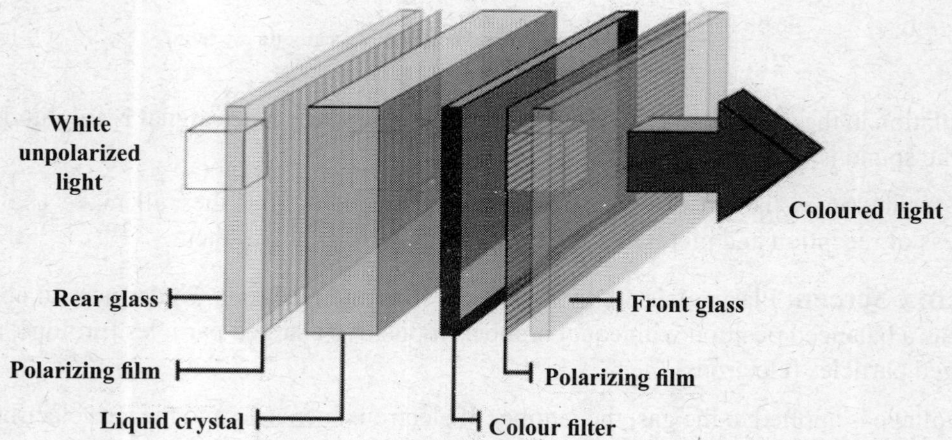

diodes (LEDs) are used as the light source. They emit brighter white light with increased picture clarity and higher contrast and they are thinner. And they consume less power.

OLED TVs: There are OLED (organic light-emitting diode) displays coming up which would be clear winners in all respects. They do not need external lighting, have high brightness and contract and lesser power but more money.

LCD vs Plasma TVs: Both LCDs and Plasma TVs have certain advantages and disadvantages. Let us look into some of them.

Life of Screen: Plasma televisions should last 10 to 20 years with normal use and the quality of the image does not degrade with time. LCD televisions may lose their quality after some years. Their life is less compared to CRTs with the present technology. High contrast levels close to 100% will reduce its life, whether it is Plasma, LCD or CRT.

Image Quality: Unlike LCDs or CRTs, image quality in plasma television does not suffer in ambient light. It will still have uniform brightness. Plasma TVs give a picture quality unmatchable by the current LCD technology. The colour saturation and contrast ratio is also better with Plasma TVs.

Viewing Angle: Plasma screens generally have a wider viewing angle than LCD. CRTs are best in this respect.

Image Lag: For high speed action, LCDs are better due to image lag.

Self-Lighting: LCD screens are backlit with a florescent light or LEDs, but on plasma screen the gas molecules emit light. CRTs of course emit their own light.

Resolution: With higher the resolution (more pixels per inch), you get better clarity particularly in case of finer details. LCD TVs beat Plasma TVs here.

Size: Plasma TVs are thinner and lighter compared to CRT televisions. But LCDs are still lighter and thinner.

Care in Handling: They are very fragile, though CRTs a little better. Plasma TVs need a little more care while shipping and handling compared to LCDs due to sensitive nature of the plasma column.

High Altitude Operation: Plasma TV cannot be successfully operated at higher altitudes. They create a noticeable buzzing sound because of the gas expansion and contraction due to the change in atmospheric pressure at high altitudes.

Power Consumption: Plasma TVs consume about 30% more power than similar LCD TV.

Care and Tips

> Good old free to air transmission and Yagi antennae dotting on the rooftops are fading out and digital transmission and satellite communication is taking over with high definition.

Quite a lot was written about the care in watching a television, the ubiquitous idiot box[50].

- ✓ Never leave televisions on while no one is watching it; you are simply burning away precious phosphors.
- ✓ Both Plasma and LCDs are subject to 'dead' pixels, which create unchanging spots on the screen. This can be a problem if you watch the same channel for very long time. The logo of the channel may burn in and make itself a permanent seat.
- ✓ Do not bend or drop these TVs. The screens are made of glass and they can become unusable in one go.
- ✓ Their surface is made up of soft and thin film which can be easily scratched. So, do not use sharp articles like spoons, screw drivers near it.
- ✓ Similarly do not spill or throw any liquids on to it or allow dust to settle on. On LCDs, the polariser may get discoloured and if the liquid enters inside it will surely spoil the circuitry.

50 Vladimir Kosma Zworykin also worked on the television, and went ahead developing better camera tubes. When asked about his favourite thing on television, he said, 'The switch. The switch to turn the damn thing off.'

✓ If you are moving these TVs from a cold air conditioned room to outside; be careful as the dew may settle on and upset the display and the circuitry.

Whether it is a CRT or LCD or plasma?

✓ Keep a watch on what your child watches and encourage him to watch those with educational value

✓ Set time limits, not more than an hour or two of television per day.

✓ Let not television take away his time of playing outside and reading.

✓ Let them not sit too close to the box.

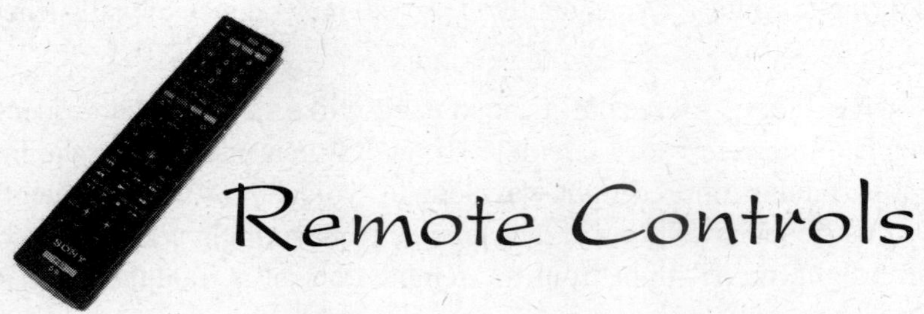

Remote Controls

We are now controlled by remote controls. I know the lady of the house used to get jittery if the gas cylinder gets empty or when her electrical grinder would not work, but now everyone gets jumpy when the remote control is missing. With the proliferation of remote controls from television to air conditioner to the music system and even opening of the garage door, they now control and command many more operations than just on and off [51].

Most remote controls for electronic appliances use infrared light. They use an infrared light emitting diode (IR LED) to emit a beam of light of about 940 nm wavelength. While we cannot see this infrared light, but the sensors in the appliance can pick it up. Video cameras and digital cameras can see this producing visible purple light.

Encoding Light: A typical remote control is alive always, but waits for a key to be pressed. When you press any key, an integrated circuit (also known as a chip) detects it. It also decodes the information, a kind of Morse code embedded into it. The code is different for each different key, and most often so with different manufacturers. The chip connects that signal to an output transistor to amplify the signal. Then the coded signal goes to an Infrared LED which emits light corresponding to the code. Your television or any other appliance has infrared sensor. The sensor receives the signal, amplifies it and sends it to the on board microprocessor which does the job as dictated by the IR signal.

Let us have a look inside a typical remote control. You have the keys on the top and in the front end a Light-emitting diode (LED). Underneath the keys is a soft rubber like panel with buttons. Each button has a black conducting dot. You have a printed circuit board below that with a few electronic components, the chip, and LED, etc. When you press a key, the conducting dots touch the board at the criss-cross copper print and make a switch contact. The chip senses that contact, generates the corresponding code in a series of pulses. A transistor amplifies and drives an IR LED.

Now when this remote control is directed towards the television or any other such appliance, the sensor receives it. These sensors do not respond to any other light other than infrared. They have range of only about 30 feet (10 meters) and they require line-of-sight. So, the infrared signal won't transmit the signal through walls or around corners; you should be able to direct in a straight line to

51 The first remote intended to control a television was developed by Zenith Radio Corporation in 1950. It was called 'Lazy Bones', which worked with a long wire. Eugene Polley developed a wireless remote control called 'Flashmatic', in 1955. It used ordinary beam of light onto a photoelectric cell, and so had its problems. In 1956, Robert Adler developed 'Zenith Space Command', a wireless remote which used ultrasound.

the device you're trying to control. Occasionally the signal may bounce of walls when it is powerful enough.

Unfortunately we have a lot of sources of infrared energy like sunlight, fluorescent bulbs and the human body which can interfere with IR remote. To avoid such interference the infrared receiver responds only to a particular infrared light wavelength, typically 980 nano-meters. Filters on the receiver pass only this frequency. To avoid interference from sunlight which also contains 980 nm wavelength infrared light, the IR light from the remote control is modulated to a frequency not present in sunlight.

The signal is amplified and fed to a microprocessor. The processor decodes the signal, processes it and initiates necessary action. The code is unique for each application, service and manufacturer and so the microprocessor does not respond to the other remote controllers. We barely realise all these interesting things that happen when we press the remote controller.

Universal Remotes: As we have already discussed, different manufacturers use different command codes to make them exclusive for their system. That makes it more complicated as you may have to handle a number of remotes. If you have a television, a satellite receiver, a DVD player and a music system, you need to work with four different remotes, even if they are from the same manufacturer. How confusing, unwieldy and frustrating! Better if you have a universal remote. For that you need to program the command codes for all the components you want to control. So now some IR remotes are pre-programmed with more than one manufacturer's command codes so they can operate multiple devices of different brands. Some remotes are programmed to learn from other remotes when you operate them[52].

52 Legendary Steve Wozniak of Apple started a company to create a remote control that could operate multiple electronic devices. Introduced in 1987, this unit known as CORE (Controller Of Remote Equipment) could 'learn' remote signals from different devices.

Radio-frequency (RF) Remotes: Radio-frequency (RF) remote controls are also very common. Car door locks and alarms, garage-door openers and radio-controlled toys are very popular now which use radio waves. They do not suffer from the line of sight problems of IR remotes. But then we are surrounded by radio waves, television, cell phones, radios and what not? They can create problems in reception, develop malfunction. Similar to IR, the problem is solved by transmitting at specific radio frequencies and encoding with specific digital address codes in the radio signal. Radio receiver then decodes only the intended signal and ignores others. RF remotes can have a range up to 100 feet and radio signals can go through walls.

Other remotes: Remotes are developed with hand-gesture recognition and voice as an alternative.

Bluetooth: While on the subject of remote controllers, let us have a few words on the Bluetooth[53] which is now very commonly used between mobile phones, telephones, laptops, personal computers, printers, Global Positioning System (GPS) receivers, and digital cameras, etc.

It is a wireless technology for exchanging data over short distances across electronic devices, with high levels of security. It can connect several devices, overcoming problems of synchronization for short distance of about 50 feet with of course low-bandwidth.

This system uses short-wavelength radio transmissions in globally unlicensed Industrial, Scientific and Medical (ISM) 2.4 GHz short-range radio frequency band.

Care and Tips

- ✓ Remote controls are delicate pieces of electronics. Do not drop or throw them. They often slip out of our hands and it is our luck they still work.
- ✓ Do not point remote controllers into the eyes of any one.

53 Bluetooth was developed in 1994 by Sven Mattisson and Jaap Haartsen, who were working for Ericsson in Sweden. It was named after Harald Bluetooth, the king of Denmark in the late 900s, who brought Denmark and part of Norway into a single kingdom.

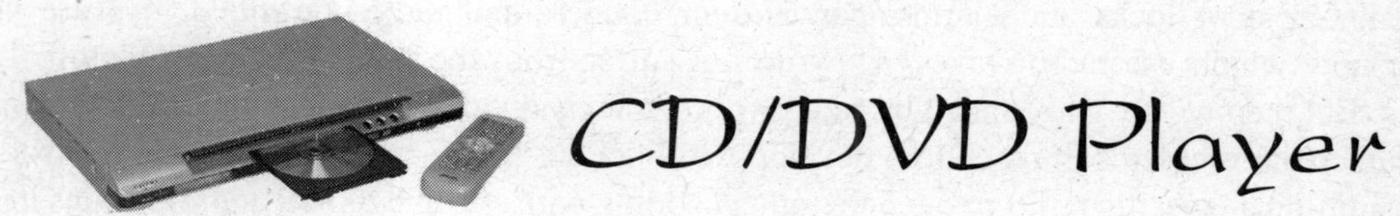

CD/DVD Player

Compact disc is a simple disc of clear polycarbonate plastic of 1.2 mm thick and 12 cm in diameter. It has an aluminium layer in the background and acrylic layer on top. That is where the simplicity ends and complexity begins. CD can store up to 74 minutes of music, at a sampling rate of 44,100 that would be mind boggling 783,216,000 bytes or 783 megabytes (MB). So, the individual bytes would be in nanometers (A nanometre is a billionth of a meter.)

Remember the gramophone playing black large long play disc, remember the reel to reel tape recorders and remember those cassette recorders. Present younger generation may not have seen the first two at all, probably the cassette recorders also. The audio recording progressed beyond recognition. Now the CDs do not only contain songs, they also can contain data, pictures, movies; anything that can be converted as bits and bytes [54].

Interestingly, CDs and DVDs follow the recording and playback method invented in 1887 by Emile Berliner[55]. Like those old gramophone records, in CDs also data is stored in a single spiral track, starting from the inside of the disc to the outside.

Bumpy Ride: During manufacturing, microscopic bumps are impressed onto this polycarbonate plastic as extremely long spiral track. Over this a thin, reflective layer of aluminium is sputtered covering the bumps. Over this a thin acrylic layer is sprayed to protect it. Then the label is printed.

The tracks are breathtakingly small, approximately 0.5 microns wide, with 1.6 microns separating one track from the next. (A micron is a millionth of a meter.) And the bumps are even more miniscule; each 0.5 microns wide, about 0.83 microns long and 125 nanometers high. (A nanometre is a billionth of a meter.) They look like pits on the aluminium side, but from the laser side, they are bumps. Look at this.

54 We normally use a decimal system of 10 numbers from 0 to 9. As the numbers progress to the left side, their value increases by 10. In a binary system they increase by two. Take the case of 1948.
Computers use two number system, also known as the binary number system. Computers or digital systems can understand only 'ON' (1) or 'OFF' (0) and all the data is entered basing this system (Binary coding or digital system). The smallest amount of transfer is one bit, either a 1, or a 0. Eight of these 'one's and/or 'zero's are called one byte. A bit is represented with a lowercase 'b,' whereas a byte is represented with an uppercase 'B'. So Kb is kilobits (actually 1024 bits), and KB is kilobytes (actually 1024 bytes). A kilobyte is eight times larger than a kilobit.

55 On November 8, 1887, Emile Berliner, patented a successful system of sound recording on flat discs or records. The first records were made of glass, later zinc, and eventually plastic. A spiral groove with sound information was etched into the flat record. The record was rotated on the gramophone. The 'arm' of the gramophone held a needle that read the grooves in the record by vibration and transmitting the information to the gramophone speaker.

The spiral track when stretched would be almost 5 km long but still 0.5 microns wide! When you think of the miniscule size of the bumps, the method of tracking, focussing and sensing the CD player needs to be exceptionally exact. To read something this small, you need an incredibly precise disc-reading mechanism.

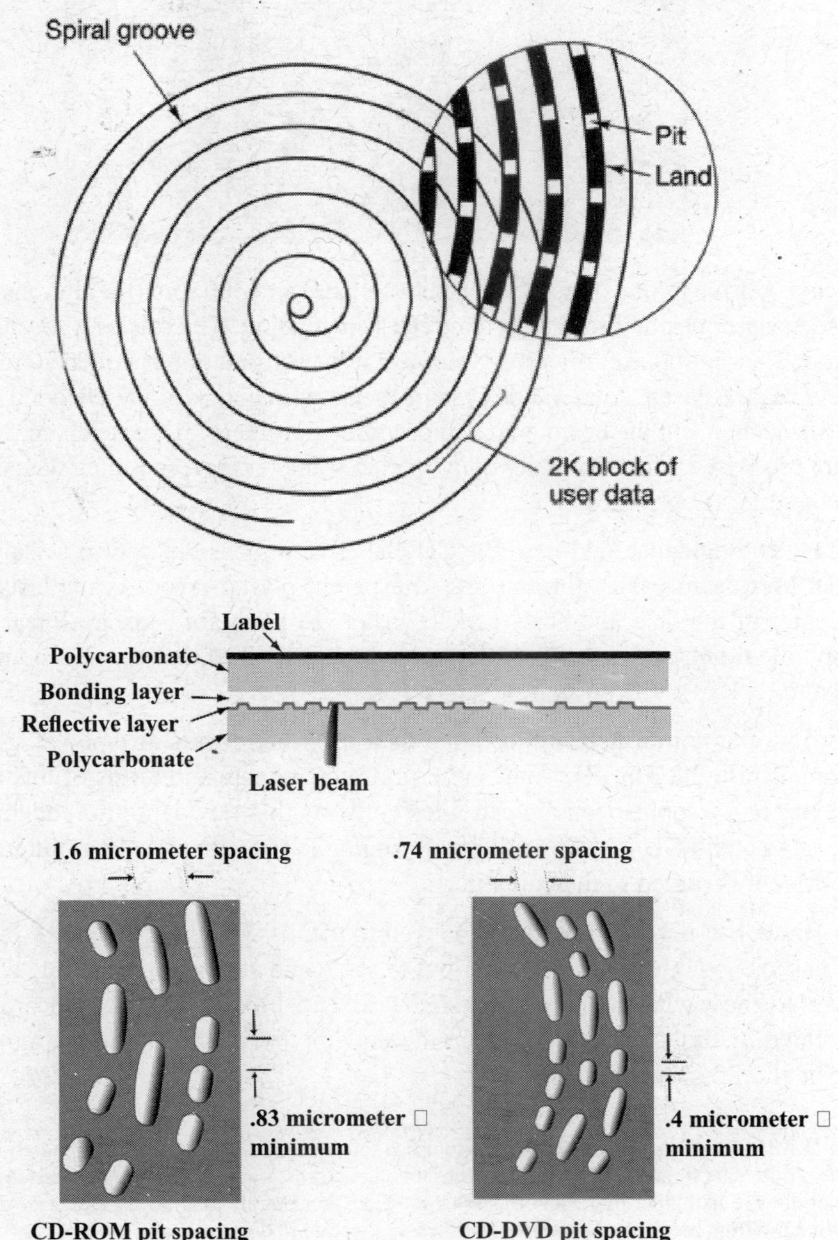

CD-ROM pit spacing

CD-DVD pit spacing

CD Player Components: Before we go further let us look what we have inside a CD player. The drive consists of a few fundamental components: a drive motor, tracking mechanism, lens system and the electronics.

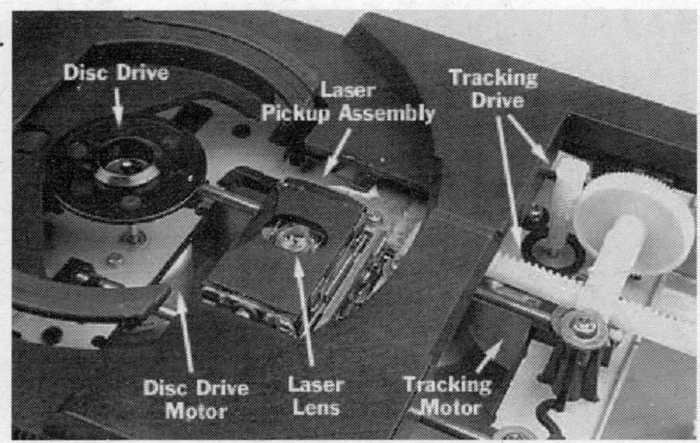

Drive Motor: A drive motor spins the disc between 200 and 500 rpm (revolutions per minute). The speed is precisely controlled to match the track it is reading. The tracking mechanism moves the lens system in a straight line at micron levels so that the information encoded along the spiral tracks is accurately read. A laser[56] and a lens system focus in on and read the encoded information. The sensor detects changes in the beam, and a microprocessor interprets these changes as binary data[57]. The data are processed, and eventually converted to sound or corresponding data using a digital-to-analogue converter (DAC) [58].

Laser Focus: The fundamental job of the CD player is to focus the laser precisely on the required track as the laser beam passes through the transparent plastic layer. As the laser moves outward from the center of the disc, the bumps move faster. To maintain constant linear speed, the drive motor or spindle motor slows down as the laser moves outward. So, the data comes off the disc at a constant rate.

Tracking: The aluminium layer reflects the data off when it hits an opto-electronic device that detects changes in light. The electronics interpret these changes in terms of bits and bytes. Inside the CD player, fairly sophisticated electronics converts this raw data into understandable format. In the case of an audio CD, it goes to digital to analogue convertors and amplifiers, in the case of a CD-ROM drive it is routed to the computer.

Date with Data: But if you think that all is well that ends well, here are a few problems a typical CD player has to encounter; we have worn-out or scratched discs, skips, missing data, misread data. We also want to know which data is where so that we can directly fetch it, or locate a particular song so that we can directly listen to it. We want to know the list of songs or data, move to it randomly or in order or shuffle or repeat.

56 The term 'LASER' is an acronym for Light amplification by Stimulated emission of radiation. Lasers emit light coherently while other light sources are incoherent. In other words, Laser beams can be focused to very tiny spots, or they do not diverge like other light sources so that they can concentrate their power at a large distance. So, they are everywhere now from medical, engineering to office application to domestic uses.

57 See footnote 54 above

58 Signals whether light or sound in the real world are analogue. We have seen in the footnote 1 that computer knows only binary language. So the voice or picture must be converted into digital signal (zeros and ones). Not only in a computer, even when you talk in a cell phone, is your voice picked up by the microphone and converted by analogue to digital convertors (ADC) before further processing and transmission. When you are listening to a voice through a speaker in your cell phone, digital to analogue convertors (DAC) does a reverse job.

To achieve this information is stored in the 'lead-in' area of the disc, which is located in an inner ring of the disc. Consuming about five kilobytes of available space, it is known as sub-code data. When you insert the disc into the drive, the message flashes, 'READING.' Yes, this is the first information that the player reads. It tells you the total number of audio tracks, play time of each track and the total or similar other data of the files you have on the CD. At the outer periphery, you have 'lead out' area which tells the player that disc has come to an end.

If the laser misreads a bump, there are error-correcting codes that detect single-bit errors and correct them. A small little speck or scratch may make CD to misread or skip, it is solved by interleaving the data. Missing bytes in music may not matter much but in the data files it means a lot, as the CD may not deliver the information at all. So, additional error correction codes are employed when it is used for data storage or as a CD-ROM.

While on the subject, there is a plethora of CD formats. CD-ROM is basically a data CD which cannot be rewritten. It is old computer term, Read Only Memory. Of late almost every new computer comes with a CD/DVD writer that can write or burn CD-R discs. CD-Rs can only be written to once and cannot be erased. Next level is CD-RW (CD-rewritable) disc that could be written and rewritten.

Drives: There are vertical, top and side and sliding tray loading mechanisms but sliding tray mechanism seems to be staying well with the consumers. There exist two types of optical tracking mechanisms, swing – arm like the old gramophones and the radial mechanism, where the lens moves radially. This is the more popular tracking now.

CD can hold about 74 minutes of audio recording or store 783 megabytes of data. This is a distinct disadvantage. Before the advent of DVDs, there were many types of CD changers that hold three or more CDs so that we can have a continuous play.

DVDs: DVDs look like the CDs and are made to the same dimensions, but they can typically contain 4.7 GB. DVDs also can store data on both sides of the device, which almost doubles their storage capacity. CDs rotate about a maximum of 500 rpm, whereas DVDs can go up to 1500 revolutions per minute. At higher rotational speed, data also can be transferred faster. Generally, the

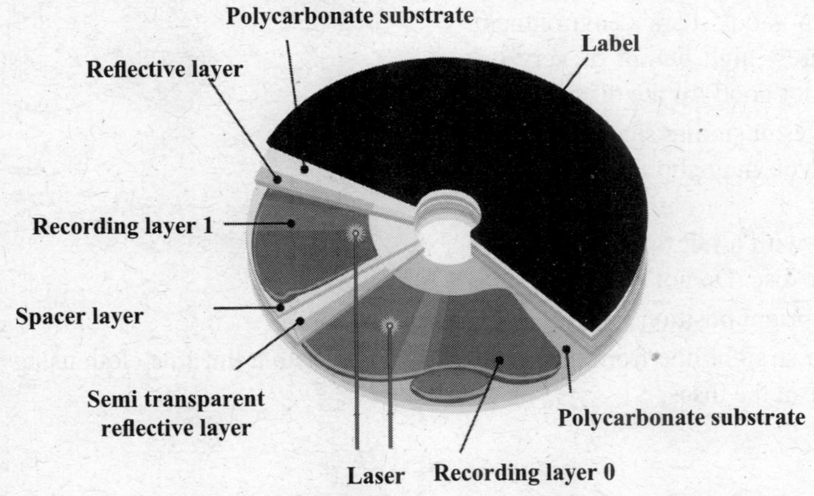

transfer rate for a CD is around 150 KB per second, but DVDs can transfer data seven times faster. If you could make the data track of a single layer of a DVD into a straight line, it would be almost 12 km or 7.5 miles long!

Burning: An intense red laser beam is focussed on to the groove. An organic dye absorbs and converts the beam's energy into heat reaching 300°C inside the groove. This temperature rise causes the plastic substrate to deform and make holes, pits and bumps. This pattern of pits and lands on a disc becomes the binary data of '0' and '1'.While playing back, the laser light falling on it reflects and opto-sensor reads it and the microprocessor processes it suitably. There are again umpteen number of DVD formats, nomenclature is similar to CDs. DVDs are available in double layer format, for instance DVD-R DL is a DVD-R with double-layer recordable disc with a capacity of 8.5 GB.

With that immense capacity if you thought DVDs will run the roost, they are being edged out by blue ray discs.

Blu Ray Disc: The Blu-ray disc, can hold up to 25 GB of data on a single-layer disc and 50 GB on a dual-layer disc and it can transfer at a speed of 36 Mbps (1x speed). It uses blue-violet laser technology (405 nm-wavelength) while DVD uses 650 nm-wavelength red laser technology.

These discs are delicate pieces of electronic marvels. They are made with a high degree of engineering insight and technological skill but cannot stand the vagaries of human error. A little care makes them last longer, after all now we store a lot of precious data in them. So..........

'Do's' and 'Don'ts' of Discs

Do

- ✓ Handle the discs by the outer edge or centre hole.
- ✓ Check the disc surface before using
- ✓ Return the discs to their cases soon after use
- ✓ Keep the discs clean and dust free.
- ✓ Store them in cool dark environment, high temperatures, high humid or very dry conditions are not good for the discs
- ✓ Do not use knives or similar sharp objectives near them lest you may slip and scratch the disc.
- ✓ Write carefully with a felt tip marker on the label side of the disc. Do not scratch.

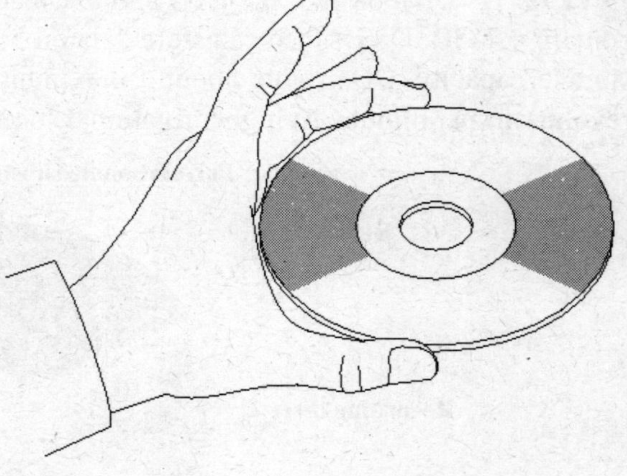

- ✓ Store discs in upright position rather than horizontally.
- ✓ Clean discs in a straight line from the centre to the edge with a lint free cloth using distilled of soft water to clean the discs.

Do not

- ✗ Touch the surface
- ✗ Bend the disc
- ✗ Open from the case only when you are ready to use.
- ✗ Expose them to prolonged Sunlight or other ultra violet sources.
- ✗ Write on the data side of the disc.
- ✗ Use a pencil, pen or fine tip marker to write
- ✗ Clean in a circular direction.
- ✗ Scratch the label side. It is softer than the other side.
- ✗ Try to peel of the original label or past another one. You are likely to unbalance the disc.

Refrigirator

Nowadays there would be a few middle class families, who do not boast a fridge, but interestingly once upon a time, large blocks of ice were shipped across continents to sell them to the rich and the shippers made a fortune, thereby.

In the present hectic life styles, the fridge is an inevitable addendum. You can keep food fresh for longer than before but still relish their freshness and nutrition, and offer chilled water and wines on a hot day or store medicines for long. Cold temperatures help food stay fresh longer and food stored at or below −18 °C is safe indefinitely but often stays good for a reasonable time at 3 to 5°C.

Well, then how the fridge works?

If you rub a drop of petrol or medical spirit on your palm, soon you'll feel the area cold! As the petrol evaporates, it absorbs the heat on the palm, making it cooler. When a liquid evaporates, it absorbs heat in the process. Air conditioner[59] also works on the same principle. The principle behind most refrigeration is that simple.

But that is where the simplicity ends. There are a number of components that work behind and inside the fridge (literally). The main components of fridge are

1. Condenser (hot coil of tubes outside the unit)
2. Evaporator (cold coil of tubes inside the fridge)
3. Expansion valve
4. Compressor
5. Refrigerant
6. Insulation

Refrigeration Cycle: The refrigerant gas is made to liquefy and evaporate, re-liquefy and evaporate again. This happens in a continuous cycle. The suitable gas[60] nowadays is R134 A, which boils at −26.3 °C (−15.34 °F). This is what happens to keep the refrigerator cool:

59 Michael Faraday was first to explain the process of refrigeration and the first known artificial Refrigeration was demonstrated by William Cullen at the University of Glasgow in 1748. Oliver Evans invented a refrigerator in 1804 in America. In 1834, Jacob Perkins invented the 'Practical Version.' In Germany Carl Paul Gottfried von Linde (1842-1934) developed refrigeration in 1876.

60 Earlier models used gases like ammonia (R-717) or sulphur di oxide (R-764) which are unsafe for domestic use. By 1915, safer, non-toxic, non-flammable Freon 12 (R-12) was introduced. Then it was realised that this gas damaged the ozone layer. So R-134A (tetrafluoroethane) gas was introduced since 1990, but R-12 is still found in many old refrigerators.

Take a look at the backside of the fridge.

1. You have a sealed compressor which compresses the gas. As the gas gets compressed or pressurised, it also heats up.
2. This high temperature, high pressure gas travels through a set of coils known as condenser. The gas cools by exposure to ambient air in the room. In the process it liquefies. This coil of tubes is visible at the back of older model fridges but presently almost all of them are enclosed for an elegant look.
3. The high-pressure liquid flows through the expansion valve. It is a special component in the tubing with a tiny hole. On side of this is high-pressure R134A liquid and on the other side is low-pressure (because the compressor is pulling the gas from that side).
4. After the expansion valve the R134A liquid reaches the evaporator which actually is the freezer compartment. The liquid actually expands or evaporates. As the liquid vaporizes, its temperature drops to −26.3 °C, in effect cooling the inside of the refrigerator.
5. The cycle repeats. A thermostat continuously senses the inside temperature of the fridge. It shuts down the motor if the temperature falls below the setting and starts again when it is high.

Parts:

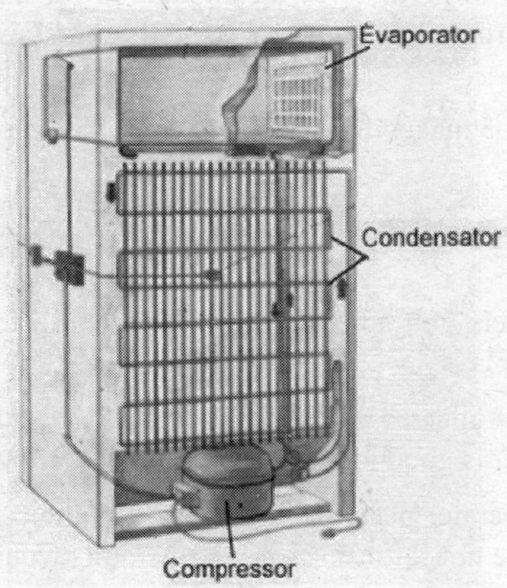

Compressor: The heart of any refrigerator or AC. The compressor is a sealed unit with motor, compressor, and gas and associated parts inside a container or shell to prevent leakage of precious gas.

Refrigerator Door: Fridge doors are lined with rubber gaskets which have magnets so as to pull the doors tight preventing ingress of external heat into the interiors of the fridge. To increase the storage space the doors have bottle and can racks on their inner side.

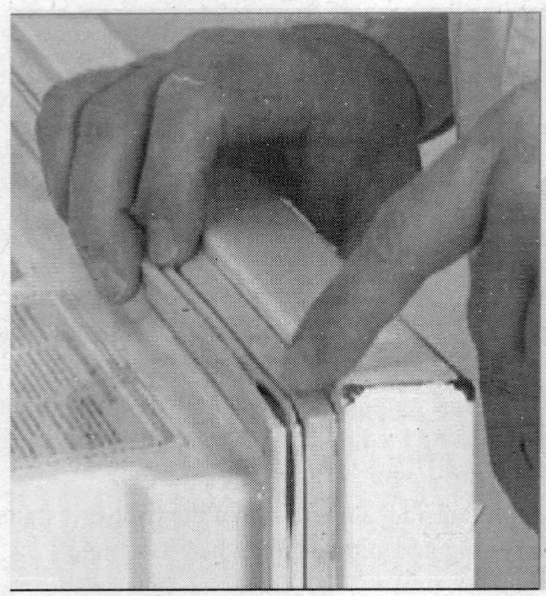

Refrigerator door gasket

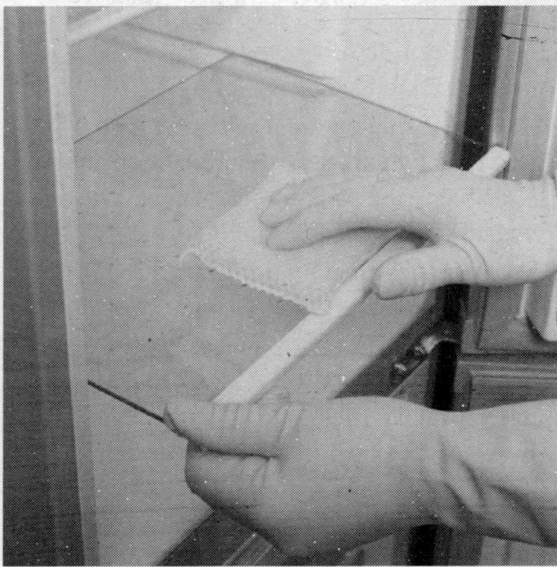

Shelf

Shelves: Entry-level refrigerators have wired shelves to permit free air circulation for uniform cooling. Shelves are adjustable to accommodate different sizes of vessels. Costlier models have toughened glass shelves.

Ice Maker: Freezer unit which is also the evaporator makes ice. Besides, you can store non-vegetarian items for longer and cooler refrigeration.

Ice Tray: Well-designed ice trays make ice quickly and also make it easy to take out the ice cubes.

Temperature Controller/Thermostat: Thermostat lets you adjust the temperatures inside the fridge. High-end models offer digital controls with displays.

Drain Pan: Excess water created from condensation is collected in a drain pan in the back side of a refrigerator. This water evaporates away naturally but it is good idea to check if it is overflowing.

Insulation: One of the key indicators of a good refrigerator performance is the insulation. In the fridge insulation keeps away the outside heat. If it were not for insulation, refrigerators would use much more energy/electricity to keep their contents cool. Polyurethane rigid foam is the widely used insulating material. It is there behind the glossy finished metal doors, sides. Because of this, modern refrigerators are at least 50% more efficient than refrigerators 20 years ago.

There are a few accessories that adorn the fridge.

Voltage Stabilizer: It is the small little box on top of the fridge. Voltage fluctuations and certainly low voltage can damage the expensive electrical parts. The voltage stabilizer regulates the voltage and saves the refrigerator from power surges and dips. Many of the modern fridges take care of these fluctuations themselves.

Fridge Stand (Pedestal): You can keep your refrigerator at a height with the fridge stand for comfortable access to fridge shelves. They improve the air circulation below the fridge and also allow you to clean the floor below your fridge.

With the basic principles [61] behind, here we have a few designs of the fridges.

Direct Cool Refrigerator: Direct cool refrigerators are the most basic types where natural convection cools the inside. So, they are energy efficient and affordable.

Frost Free Refrigerator: Frost free models feature electric fans to circulate cool air inside to prevent formation of ice. In turn they also keep uniform temperature inside it. There are further variations in the frost free refrigerators:

Single Door Refrigerator: These are entry-level refrigerators, in the low-price range, with a small footprint and in the capacity of around 50-300 litre.

Double Door Refrigerator: Double door fridges in the range of about 200-600 litres are becoming more fashionable. Top door covers the freezer compartment while the bottom door seals the fridge compartments. We frequently open the general compartment; hence ingress of heat goes less into freezer which operates at sub-zero temperature.

Side-by-side Refrigerator: These are higher end models with large capacities say 800 litre. They feature side-by-side doors just like that of a cupboard. Some models have water dispensers where you can fill your glass without opening any door. They save on energy as only one–half of the door opened normally.

Bottom Mounted Refrigerator: This is a unique ergonomic design where the freezer is fixed at the bottom and the fridge section is on the upper side. In the general models you have the vegetable basket at the bottom and the freezer at the top. So, you need stoop to get a fruit or a vegetable. This model eliminates that problem.

- **Star Rating** : Thanks to recent improvements in insulation and compressors, today's refrigerators use much less energy than older models. You will find a label with stars on a fridge. That's the Energy efficiency rating label. The more stars on the label, the more energy efficient the appliance is compared to similar models. These labels also show annual energy consumption (kWh per year), calculated on average expected use over a year.

Care and Tips

A little care helps you to improve the service and life of the fridge.

✓ Keep the door seal clean. Replace old and worn door seals with new.

✓ Always keep the door shut. The more you open the door the more heat goes inside and fridge works harder. Some of the modern fridges sound an alarm if the door is kept open longer.

61 There other interesting methods of cooling. Peltier coolers are solid state and smallest refrigerators. Magnetic refrigerators work on the magnetocaloric effect. The cooling effect is triggered by placing a metal alloy in a magnetic field. Acoustic refrigerators use compressed helium gas and resonant linear reciprocating motors/alternators to generate a sound that is converted to heat and cold as. The heat is discarded and the cold is routed to the refrigerator.

- ✓ One of the major problems with a fridge is that ice builds up on the freezer unit which prevents it from doing its further good work. Ice is essentially a bad conductor of heat so it impedes further heat transfer or cooling. Defrost the compartment when the ice reaches 1.5 cm thick. If it is thicker the fridge will use more electricity than necessary. So it is essential to remove the ice from time to time manually or automatically. Presently, most of the higher end models feature automatic defrosting.
- ✓ Do not overload shelves, as they could break. Incidentally, empty fridge consumes more power.
- ✓ If the coils are dusty, your fridge will work harder, increasing your power bills. But they are delicate.
- ✓ Do not keep heavy items on the door shel[illegible] they will put the door hinges under stress.
- ✓ Adjust the thermostat for proper temperatur[illegible]ending on the contents of food.
- ✓ Check the drain pot quite often and clean the [illegible]ain every few months with a cotton swab.

And if you wish to transport the refrigerator please follow these guidelines.

- ✓ Turn refrigerator off a few hours before moving to allow the evaporator to defrost.
- ✓ Remove all foods and clean inside.
- ✓ If the travel time is longer, place a small bag of activated charcoal [illegible] carbon inside the refrigerator to absorb odours.
- ✓ Secure loose items, such as the grille, shelves, storage pans, ice trays, ice storage bucket.
- ✓ Cover the exterior with a blanket and secure it. It is best to keep it standing upright while transporting.
- ✓ Handle with care.

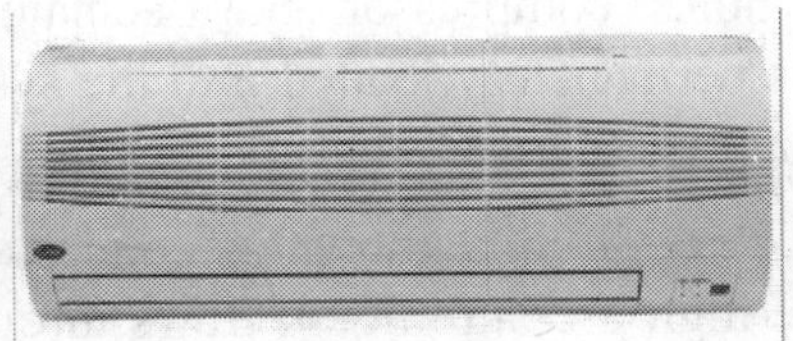

Air Conditioner

Air conditioners are very much similar to refrigerators. Only difference is that the refrigerator cools what is inside a box whereas the AC cools the atmosphere outside. In practice, Air conditioners condition the room temperature irrespective of the outside weather, and in the process they remove excess moisture from the room or they dehumidify the room. They create a pleasant atmosphere in our room to work our best or feel relaxed. Air conditioning is also used in certain manufacturing applications where the process air is conditioned suitable for the process application.

Well, then how the air conditioner works?

It works on the same principles[62] as a refrigerator.

If you rub a drop of petrol or medical spirit on your palm, soon you'll feel the area cold! As the petrol evaporates, it absorbs the heat on the palm, making it cooler. When a liquid evaporates, it absorbs heat in the process. We need a refrigerant gas which can be evaporated, liquefied and evaporated again in a cycle. Ammonia was one such gas which was used originally but was soon discontinued as it is dangerous for domestic use. Later, Freon was the gas for decades but now it is being discontinued because of its drastic environmental effects. The suitable gas nowadays is R134 A. You have the same parts as a fridge but now with fans to suck hot air and blow cold air.

If you draw out a window air conditioner, you will see the parts shown in this picture.

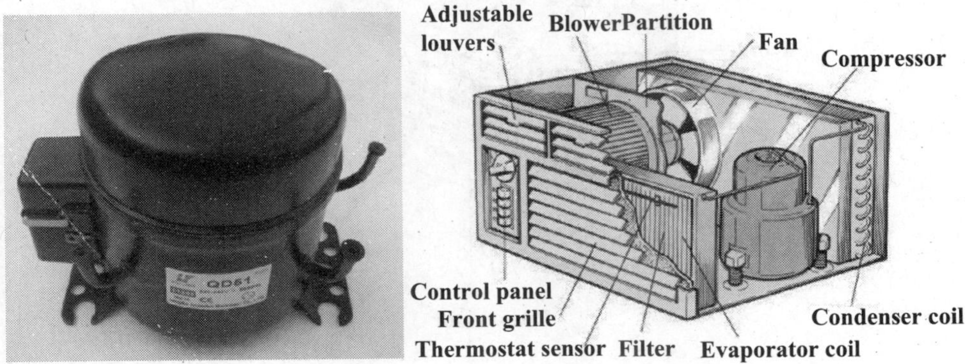

62 In 1820, British scientist and inventor Michael Faraday discovered that when the liquefied ammonia was allowed to evaporate it could chill air. The first large-scale electrical air conditioning was invented by Willis Haviland Carrier in 1922.

You have a sealed compressor which contains the gas, motor, compressor and associated parts along with the evaporator and condenser coils. The gas is permanently loaded into the system to avoid losses due to leaks, etc. As the gas gets compressed or pressurised, it also heats up.

This high temperature, high pressure gas passes through a set of coils known as condenser. The gas is cooled by a fan and in the process it liquefies. The high-pressure liquid flows through the expansion valve. After the expansion valve the R134A liquid reaches the evaporator which is a unit with series of finned tubes. You can see it in the front if you open the filter. As the liquid actually expands or evaporates, its temperature drops. Hot air from the room is sucked in here through the grill and filters, which gets cooled in effect. Cold air is blown back into the room through ducting and adjustable louvers. The cycle repeats. A thermostat continuously senses the temperature at the evaporator. It shuts down the motor if the temperature falls below the setting and starts again when it is high. Modern ACs employ digital controls for setting temperature, fan speed, timer and a lot of other facilities.

Other than the basic evaporator, condenser, etc. AC also has a few more important parts. Let us have a look at them.

Air Filters: Air filters trap dust, and other airborne particles before it enters the AC unit for our better health and hygiene. They also increase the life of ACs by keeping dust away.

Drain Pan: In the process of dehumidification, AC units produce a significant amount of water which collects in the drain pan and is drained out through a tube. Please make sure that it is not plugged.

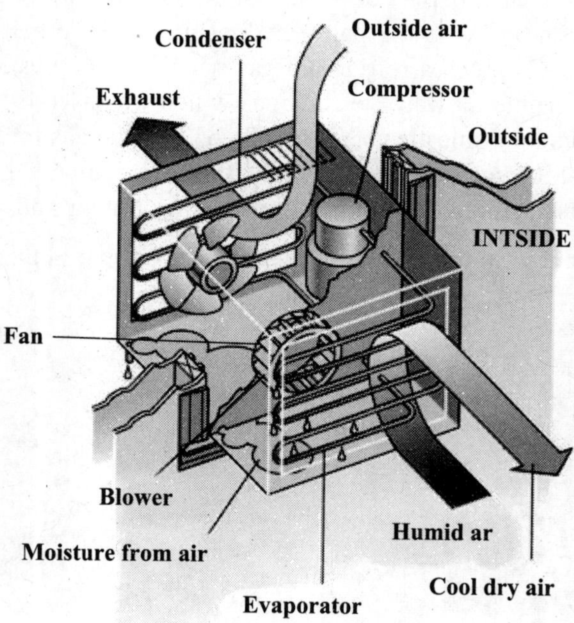

Remote: Remote controller helps you to control the unit without going near the main unit. Apart from setting the temperature, modern ACs feature a few more interesting features built into it.

New Avatars: Good old window AC is donning new Avatars and soon may be obsolete. Let us look into some of the models.

Windows AC: Window ACs have all the components inside a box which snugly fits into a window opening, making it easy for installation and costs less in comparison to other varieties[63].

Split AC: Split AC is a two piece AC with the indoor unit installed inside a room which cools the room and takes out warm air. This external unit throws away the warm air. It also contains the compressor, etc. and is connected to the internal unit with the gas piping and electric cables. This model improves the home décor, and is more silent. Internal unit takes up less space for installation and can be installed in room with no windows.

Tower AC : It is used for high capacity cooling, intended for large rooms at home and in offices. They do not need windows or wall installation.

Cassette AC:These are shaped like cassettes and are designed to be installed on ceilings.

Cube Air Conditioner: This is a fairly new design which can be mounted close to a ceiling or at the window level.

We often hear terms like 1 ton or 1.5 ton ACs. Fortunately it is not the weight of the AC unit. Capacity of ACs is measured in British Thermal Units or BTUs. (A BTU is approximately the amount of heat you get from burning one kitchen match all the way down.)[64] Approximately we may need 30 BTUs per square foot. The energy efficiency rating (EER) indicate how efficient is your AC. Preferably EER should be as high as possible but would be available at a higher cost.

Air conditioners with 1 Ton capacity are suitable for small rooms of approximately 8" × 10" rooms while those of 1.5 Ton capacity are suitable for medium size rooms of say, 12" × 15" floor.

Care and Tips

- ✓ Dirt is the biggest enemy of air conditioners, more so for window units; it can block the filter, reduce the efficiency of the evaporator coil, and clog drain ports.
- ✓ However the coils, the compressor, and the motor of a room air conditioner are sealed components, so any repairs to them should be left to a professional service person. Any small mistake can incur huge expenses.
- ✓ Before doing any work on a room air conditioner, make sure it is unplugged.
- ✓ **Filter:** At the beginning of every summer and once a month during the season, clean the filter. It can often be removed by taking out the front grill. Clean the filter with soap solution or mild household detergent and water. Let it dry fully before fixing it back.
- ✓ **Power Cord:** Place the power cord carefully so that it does not dangle, get cut or damaged.
- ✓ **Evaporator and Condenser Coils:** Similarly it is a good idea to clean the evaporator and condenser coils at the beginning of every summer and once a month during the season. Use a vacuum cleaner on these components. You may have to take professional help for doing this

63 In 1945, Robert Sherman of Lynn invented window air conditioner. A large manufacturer stole the idea. Sherman was not rich enough to fight the big company in court and they threatened to 'break him' if he tried.

64 Heat required to melt one pound of ice is measured as 144 BTU or it takes a ton duty equivalent to 12,000 BTU per hour. So, a 1.5 ton of cooling effect is equal to 18,000 BTU/hour.

and you have to be careful. Thermostat tubing is delicate which is positioned in front of the evaporator. Be careful not to damage it.

✓ **Drain Ports:** As the air conditioner works, it dehumidifies or picks up moisture from the air. This water is drained out through a hole and tube. This drain port can get clogged with dirt. Then the water leaks from other places and stagnant water can smell and rust the steel. Clean the port with a short piece of wire or similar.

Caution

- Air conditioners are prone for theft and window ACs create an access for the robber. Please be careful about it.
- Voltage fluctuations are biggest enemy of an AC. Low voltages can burn the motors as well as high voltages. As most of the motors are sealed units, it will be required to evacuate and fill the gas again. So, the repairs are expensive. Voltage stabilisers are used traditionally but modern ACs can handle wide range of voltages. But low voltage can damage as much as high voltage.
- Please understand that the air in AC is circulated. So, spending most of the time in AC environment is not advised because of the reduced free supply of oxygen over a period. You may also feel dryness of mucous membranes in the nose and mouth.

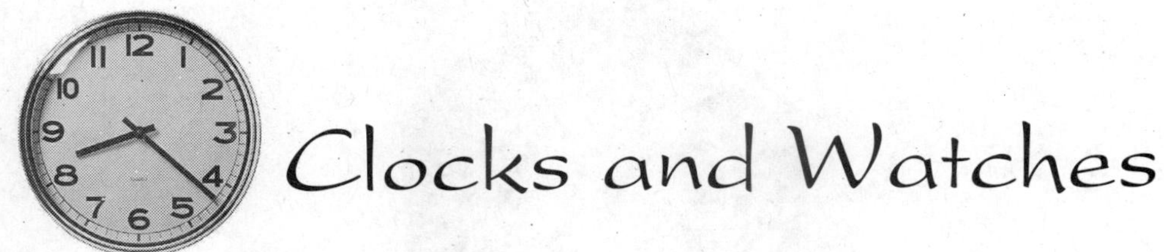

We once used the Earth's rotation to measure time, where one spin equates to a day. The day began with the Sun rising and closed with nightfall. But the time was accurate by the hour. Our earth wobbles on its axis as it rotates, some days can be shorter or longer than others. For centuries, time was measured by sand clocks or water clocks.

Then came the weight driven or spring driven pendulum clocks, in that order and then the table clocks with alarm. Wrist watches were the next thing around; watches with day date came next. They all had the drudgery of winding periodically. A little later the rich and the stylish started flaunting their self-winding watches.

Digital era threw all these watches out from their mantle pieces or handsome wrists and lovely arms.

Most of the present generation may not have seen majestic pendulum clocks that adorned the drawing halls or those wonderful time pieces carefully kept on the tables. They are now mostly decorative pieces kept for their antique value. I still do not understand why we have forsaken those environmentally friendly devices and got to these clocks which tax our natural resources.

Grandfather Clocks: Pendulum clocks stood tall, and elegant in our drawing rooms for almost 300 years [65], until the invention of the quartz clock in 1927. By1970, quartz clocks have virtually evicted the pendulum clocks and wind up clocks. Before we take up the quartz clocks, let us have a look at the grandfather clocks.

So, we had to wind up these big clocks once in a week and the table clocks once a day. Forget it, the clock stops and you have to search for another clock to know the correct time and set this one. There was even an earlier version of pendulum clocks where you had to pull a weight to keep it going.

Table clock or drawing room clock is a miracle of mechanical engineering. Even though the clock looks complicated when you open it, there are a few basic parts.

- **Weight or spring** provides the energy or the power to turn the hands of the clock. You pull a weight with a set of pulleys; it slowly falls and turns a set of gears. On the other hand, a spring is wound with a key and as it unwinds, it turns a set of gears.
- **Weight gear train** – increases the number of revolutions and transfer them to the pendulum.

65 Around 1602 Galileo discovered that the time taken for a pendulum to go back and forth once (pendulum swing) is related only to the length of the pendulum and the force of gravity and not its weight. The Dutch astronomer Christian Huygens applied this principle to invent the clock in 1656 and patented it in the next year.

- **Escapement** is a mechanism which engages and disengages and gives the pendulum timed impulses to keep it swinging. Tick-Tick sound from the clock generates here.

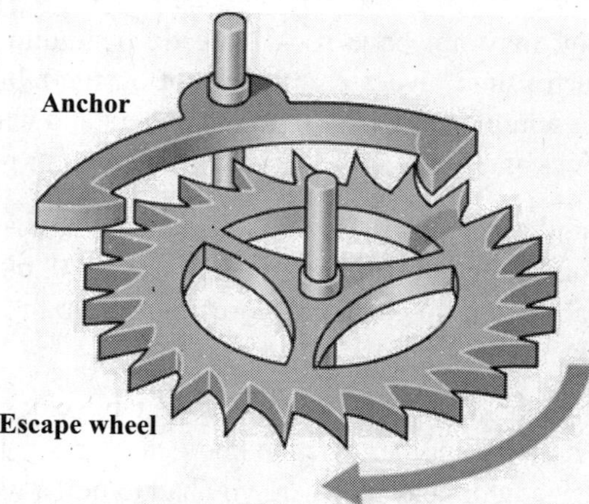

- **Pendulum** with a weight on a rod is the principle time keeping which moves to and fro.
- **Hand gear train** consists of gears to move the minute and hour hands turn correctly.
- An **indicator or dial** is the traditional clock face with rotating hands with twelve digits imprinted on it. This characteristic imprint is often referenced to indicate the position of an object, say 3 O'clock, 10 O'clock position, etc. Minutes and seconds hands have coaxial shafts to turn them on. Some clocks seconds hand is fixed on a subsidiary dial.
- **Setting mechanism** helps in time setting and correcting. Because all of these gears are engaged to each other, you cannot rewind or set the clock. This mechanism disengages the gear train

when we do so. When you pull a small button on your wristwatch to set the time, this is what precisely happens.

They Had Their Problems: But these clocks had their problems which were solved as they evolved over time.

Thermal compensation: An increase in temperature causes the pendulum rod to expand, makes it longer. So, the period of oscillation increases and the clock loses time.

Atmospheric drag: Atmospheric drag also affects the pendulum swing.

Levelling : To keep time accurately, pendulum clocks must be absolutely level.

Gravity: Gravity can change the pendulum, so pendulum clocks must be readjusted to keep time after a moving to a far away new place.

Most of these clocks had to be wound once in a week or so and they worked well for years. Then they visited the mechanic's place for 'over-oiling' (mechanic's word for overhauling).

Then came the table clocks. But these clocks did not have pendulums, so they use an oscillating wheel in place of a pendulum, which provides the precise time base.

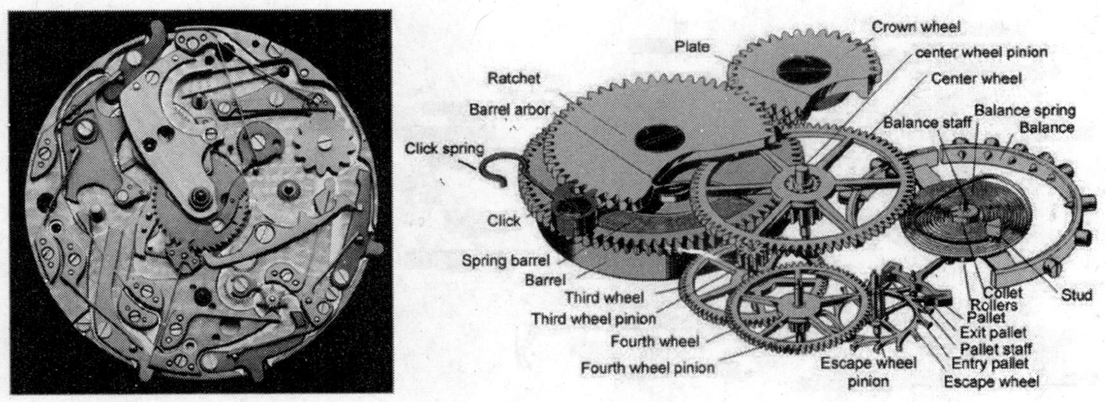

Wind-up alarm clocks are wonderful pieces of mechanical engineering and a ladies watch is pure magic of miniaturisation. Right from the 14th Century, interesting innovations made the watches[66] smaller, thinner, more reliable, more accurate and even self-winding (at the sleight of your hand)!

Table Clocks and Wrist Watches: Watches and table clocks have almost the same components as the bigger clocks, only watches are smaller. Additionally, table clocks have spring, gears and settings, and hammers for the alarm.

An internal spiral mainspring powers the watch. Spring is wound with the help of a small knob at the side. After the winding is full, the ratchet clicks, over-winding is prevented. As the spring unwinds, a gear train is set in motion. Taking power from the main spring a balance wheel moves right and left, driving one gear tooth at a time. In effect balance wheel gives the time base. The

66 In 1504, the first portable timepiece was invented in Nuremberg, Germany by Peter Henlein. French mathematician and philosopher, Blaise Pascal (1623-1662) was probably the first person to wear a watch.

balance wheel has a hair spring which controls the rate of oscillations precisely reversing it. Escape mechanism is connected to the balance wheel and is the origin of tick-tick sound of the watch. From here, the movement is connected to a number of gears and pinions which drive the hours, minutes and seconds' hands, and also the day date indications if there are any. The gear spindles are held in position by jewels to prevent wear out due to constant movement. The more number of jewels, the costlier the watch and more durable. As the main spring unwinds, it loses its energy and you have to rewind it again. Forget it; it stops probably after a day, in some watches after two days. That's a problem and led to the invention of a self winding watch[67].

Automatic Watches: I said 'sleight of hand' in an earlier paragraph which winds the watch. True. We continuously move our hands more or less. This movement of hand is translated into winding the watch.

Look at the picture. The watch has an eccentric weight or rotor mounted on a pivot, half-round piece covering the inside watch. Our hand movements make the rotor move on its pivot. These movements are in turn connected to a ratcheted winding mechanism with a series of gears and pinions. These watches can store energy for almost two days so you need not keep shaking your hand while at sleep. Of course, they can also be wound manually. A slipping mechanism prevents the watch from excess winding, probably meant for politicians making wild speeches!

Alarm Clock[68]: There is another spiral spring for the alarm and set of gears. A key winds the alarm spring and slips as it gets fully wound. Another knob sets the alarm time. There is small

67 Swiss John Harwood invented the self-winding watch in 1923.

68 Greeks were using alarm clacks even around 250 BC. They built a water clock with raising waters to keep time. When they hit a mechanical bird, whistle was sounded. Levi Hutchins of Concord, New Hampshire, invented the first mechanical alarm clock in 1787, but that would ring only at 4 AM. Seth E Thomas patented a mechanical wind-up alarm clock that could be set for any time on October 24, 1876.

secondary dial or alarm hand to set the time. The alarm goes off when the preselected 'wake-up' time synchronises with the actual time. A hammer is released which strikes a bell giving out the sound. Later models had a snooze knob when pressed the alarm will ring again after a few minutes, say 8 minutes.

With the advent of digital clocks, these older clocks may be out of fashion but they are not out of circulation. They are still the choice for heavy sleepers and still the best bet if you want work with renewable resources.

Digital Clocks

The problem with pendulum clocks, table clocks and wrist watches is that you have to wind them from time to time. If you forget, they stop. And you have the temperature and gravity problems, which gave rise to an old adage, 'No two watches agree!' They are now kept mostly for their decorative and antique value.

Though their principles were discovered in the late twenties, 'quartz watch' burst onto the scene only during the 1970s[69]. They are powered by small silver oxide batteries which last several years. They are surprisingly more accurate and fairly cheaper. They still have the gear train that counts the seconds, minutes, and hours. But the time base comes from a tiny quartz crystal instead of a swinging pendulum or a moving balance wheel. These functions are handled electronically rather than mechanically.

Mr Crystal: Quartz crystal is a small little electronic marvel, made from silicon dioxide (silicon is the stuff from which computer chips are made.) It is piezoelectric. When compressed or bent, it generates a voltage on its surface. Reverse is also true and if a voltage is applied, quartz will bend or change its shape very slightly. Using these principles, quartz crystals are used in the clocks and

69 Probably the first truly digital wrist watch was made by American manufacturer Hamilton Watch Company in 1972, made of 18-carat gold, costing $2,100. It was a glowing red LED display which was activated by pressing a button on the side. However, a digital clock appeared in the 1968 movie '2001: A Space Odyssey,' made by Stanley Kubrick.

watch to create accurate time base. The crystal is made to vibrate at a frequency exactly 32,768 times each second.

This frequency is divided to generate one second pulses. It is similar to mechanical clocks; gears divide the main time base there, and here the electronic circuits accomplish that. An amplifier amplifies these pulses to drive a small electric motor. In fact, it is a coil of copper wire acting as a solenoid which drives a gear train. Further the gear train consists of appropriate gears and pinions to move the hour, minutes and seconds hands. Another simple gear train provides for the alarm for setting and operating it. When the time movement synchronizes with the alarm set gear, the alarm goes off via a piezo buzzer.

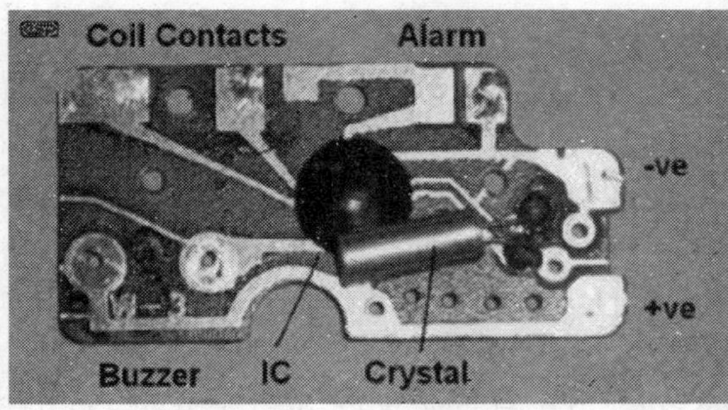

Clocks with digital displays have become common place nowadays as they directly show the time either by LEDs (light emitting diodes) or an LCD (liquid crystal display). Crystal frequency base is standard, but now it is still higher in the order of 3.58 MHz or 358000000 cycles per second. This frequency is divided to give one second pulses, minutes and hours. All the numbers from 0 to 9 can be configured in seven segments which is a common practice in digital displays. Look here for instance.

As the time advances, electronic circuitry drives the segments correspondingly. These clocks can show the time in 12 hour clock mode or 'the railway time,' 24 hour clock. In 12 hour mode display shows AM or PM.

To set the clock most clocks have 'fast' and 'slow' set buttons. When you press the 'fast' button, digits move faster and in the slow button the digits move slower but much faster than normal time. This is most common time setting method.

Alarm time is also set in similar fashion. When the set time synchronizes with the actual time, alarm goes off. Alarm can be put off by another button. We have an additional snooze feature, where we can make the alarm to repeat after few minutes.

Inverters

Inverters have become an inevitable necessity in average domestics because of unreliable power supplies. Power is simply not available, come on and go off at the whims and fancies of the electricity boards; when it is available either the voltage is high or low.

As we have seen in earlier chapter, the domestic supply is alternating current at 230Volts. And we cannot store it. We have also seen that batteries can store electric power but it is direct current. So, we need to have a system where we can store power from the mains when it is available into the battery and take it back when the domestic power is not available.

It is like a bank where we keep our savings and take it back when we need it. Only difference is that banks do it in rupee to rupee transaction normally but here it is a little more complicated; we will not enter into complications though. AC voltage must be transformed to a lower level and converted to DC so that it can be stored in a battery. Next, DC available with the batteries must inverted back to AC before it can be fed into our domestic lines. So the inverter that sits innocuously in the corner of our homes, the little black box does a whole lot of things. It has to cope with a wide range of loads, from a single night light to a sudden load; it has to manage wide voltage variations that continuously bother the domestic supply. Still it has to regulate its quality within narrow constraints, with a minimum of power loss. This is a tall task.

Let us look into the working of inverters briefly. The storage of power is by batteries; very common is lead acid batteries of 12V, though 24V batteries are used more and more because of higher power demands. 230V AC voltages is now stepped down or transformed to 12V. This alternating voltage is then rectified or converted to direct current. Now, this DC voltage is used to charge the battery, in other words store it. This voltage needs to be fed carefully into the battery with appropriate current so that it is not overcharged or left undercharged. Storage capacity of batteries is given in ampere – hours.

Now to feed the storage back to our mains, two things must happen; it must be changed from direct current to alternating current and it should be stepped up to 230 volts. The alternating current in our mains is a true sine wave. It runs smoothly up and down in a wave-like motion at 50 cycles per second. Sine wave is clean and smooth, like a swinging pendulum. It is the ideal form of AC power. That is where the problem starts. With conventional electronic circuits it is difficult to achieve pure sine wave.

Square Wave-sine Wave: Electronic circuits can easily make square waves but square wave units are not efficient and could be harmful to some electronic equipment. They are virtually on their way out, like the horse carriages on the highways. The most common and cheaper inverters make modified sine wave. It is actually a modified square wave with the corners suitably trimmed. They are also known as Quasi sine wave output inverters. Even with this kind of waves many of our household equipment cannot work properly. A buzz will be heard from the speakers of the audio systems, fluorescent lights, ceiling fans, and transformers may also give out this annoying buzz. Microwave ovens, TVs and computers may not tolerate this. Although Modified sine wave power inverters are more portable, lighter, and less costly, and scientifically designed to somewhat simulate pure sine wave output, they do not offer the same 'perfect' electrical output. Actually a sine wave inverter can deliver cleaner, more stable power than most grid connections. For any sensitive equipment, it is advisable to use a pure sine wave inverter. Presently many of the inverters produce pure Sine wave with the help of advanced Digital signal processing (DSP) techniques. Micro controllers monitor and control various applications sand parameters. Presently MOSFETs are used to drive the final outputs efficiently.

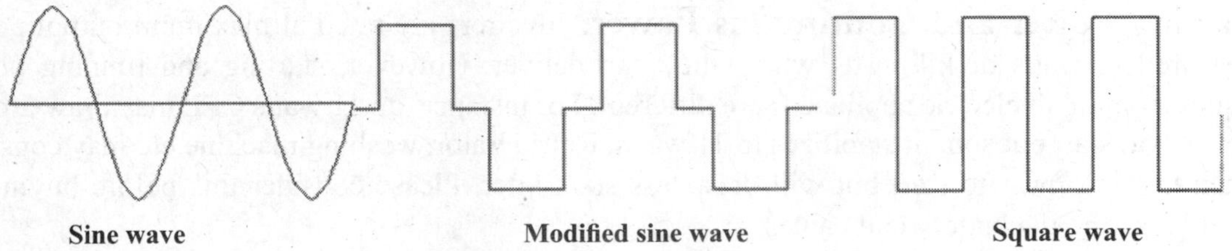

Batteries: Battery is the vital part of inverter as the performance and life of an inverter is greatly depends upon battery. Lead acid batteries are the most common types of batteries for use with inverters. They feature not only a low energy to weight ratio but also can offer high discharge current. These batteries are undergoing a number of developments in the recent years like flooded lead acid, tubular, sealed maintenance free batteries, etc. Batteries are rated in ampere-hours for their rated capacity.

Automotive lead acid batteries cannot be used successfully in the inverters as they are not designed for discharges by more than 25% of their rated capacity. So inverters use deep cycle batteries. A deep cycle battery provides a steady current over a long period of time, and they can also provide a surge current when needed. They can be deeply discharged over and over again down to 80%. To accomplish this, these batteries use thicker plates. Tubular batteries charge faster and last longer. They are more efficient, and extremely strong, so as to stand longer power cuts.

Maintenance Free Batteries : Lead acid batteries require regular maintenance. The electrolyte level must be checked and topped up at regular intervals. You should keep the batteries in a ventilated place and also protect the terminals free from corrosion and build up. Maintenance free batteries are sealed lead acid batteries. They do not require check-up, top up or additional ventilation. However they are costlier and their life shorter.

Inverter or Home Ups?: Inverter inverts Direct current from battery to Alternating current as a backup power generating device in case of mains power failure. UPS as the name suggests provides uninterrupted power supply to equipment. Functionally, both inverter and UPS do the same job. The difference is in the switching time. Switching over time of a UPS is typically 3 to 5 milliseconds only, but for an inverter takes it is around 500 milli seconds which is unacceptable for the electronics devices like computers. UPSs are further classified as; offline, online and line interactive. Home UPS are normally offline only; hence they cannot be used to drive sophisticated devices.

Grid-tied Inverter: A Grid-Tied inverter synchronises with existing mains electricity supply. This type of inverter allows you to tie your spare electricity say from solar cells into the grid system.

Protection : Many of the better designed inverters offer a number of alarms, trips and indications of faults either as audio visual indications or alphanumeric displays. Overloads can be due to simply too much load for the inverter at that time or faulty appliance, or a wiring fault, etc. Battery may be fully charged or over discharged, etc. Several sensors accomplish this in conjunction with microcontrollers. For instance a low voltage alarm will sound when the battery voltage falls below 10 volts and even shutdown the inverter.

Starting Power and Continuous Power: Inverters are rated at maximum output power measured in watts or kilowatts which they can deliver. However, starting and running power requirement of all electric appliances are different. For instance, an 11 watts CFL may draw around 15 watts to start but soon it stabilizes to 11 watts. Refrigerator, washing machine etc may consume much higher power to start but will draw less soon after. Please consider this before buying an inverter, sizing the battery and cables.

Wattage Rating of Home Appliances: The capacity of your inverter is dependent on the load you will require to power. Almost all AC electrical equipment nowadays will bear a label indicating how many amps or watts of electricity it consumes. Here, is also a rough indication how much our common electrical appliances consume.

Appliances	Power
Fan (Ceiling)	50-75 watts
Fan (Table)	25-50 watts
CFL 18 watts	18 watts
Computer (Desktop)	80- 150 watts
Laptop	20- 75 watts
LCD TV (32')	150 watts
Refrigerator	160 – 250 watts
Tube Light (4 Feet)	40 watts

Difference between VA and Watts: Manufacturers confuse and mislead the consumers with watts and VA ratings of inverter or other home appliances. Power in watts is the real power drawn and VA is the apparent power. The ratio of power in watts to power in VA is termed as Power factor. Unfortunately, manufacturers often don't specify the power factor or efficiency in their products. Simply speaking, an inverter with VA rating will be able to supply less power in watts. If an inverter or UPS is coming without mentioning power factor, you must take a safe value of 0.6 (60%) as power factor while connecting appliances.

Battery Backup: Batteries are rated by their ampere hours and their voltage. 12 volt battery rated at 150 ampere-hours (AH) can deliver 1800 watts in one hour or 900 watts for two hours and so on, though they may not discharge high currents at this rate. We can calculate how long the battery would last when the power fails from the following formula. Actual time depends on the battery condition and accumulated losses and may taper off in the end.

Time (in hrs) = <u>Battery voltage (in volts) * Battery capacity (in Ah)*efficiency of inverter</u>
Load (in VA)

Let us have a sample calculation

Battery voltage = 12 Volts

Battery Capacity = 150 Ah

Load = One fluorescent lamps (40 watts) and one ceiling fan (75 watts)= 115 watts

Inverter efficiency = 80%= 0.8

Backup Time = 12 * 150*0.8/115= 12.5 hrs (Approx)

Care and Tips

- ✓ Keep them in a cool dry place.
- ✓ Keep them away from liquids or condensing humidity.
- ✓ Keep them well-ventilated. Allow at least 1 inch of clearance around the unit for air flow. Ensure that ventilation openings on the bottom and rear of the unit are not blocked.
- ✓ Keep the inverter just away from the batteries and never install it in the same compartment.
- ✓ But install it as close to the battery as possible keeping the above point in mind). Minimize the length of wire from the inverter to the battery. Longer AC wires are better than longer DC cables.
- ✓ Position the inverter as far as possible from the television, the antenna and the antenna cables if interference is seen in the TV or buzzing in some audio-equipment. Adjust the orientation as required.

Passenger Elevators or Passenger Lifts

Think of the anger and anxiety in the office going man's eyes when the lift does not come up in time or someone forgets to close the door properly or simply the power fails. Think again, when you return from office tired and lift stops at seventh floor and you live in eighth floor. With more and more apartments in multi-storeyed complexes coming up, elevators or lifts have become an everyday affair. By the way Americans call it an elevator and the British call it a lift[70]. We talk like British but ape for the Americans. So let us go to an elevator.

A passenger elevator consists of a car or cab where people can stand and travel up or down. It is pulled up by means of rolling steel ropes or by hydraulic cylinders. The car travels in an enclosed space called a shaft or hoistway.

Traction Elevator: Traction elevators are by far the most common and they are several variations to them depending on the need. In the traction elevators, the car is raised and lowered by traction steel wires. An electric motor is located in the machine room up above the elevator shaft. It drives a gear box which reduces the speed of the motor and increases its torque. Hoisting pulley or sheave is fixed here over the output which the wire ropes are looped around. As the pulley rotates the ropes travel on it. There may be four or six steel ropes which travel all the way down to the cab. They are wound around a driven pulley on the car. The other ends of the cables are attached to a counterweight that moves up and down in the side of the elevator shaft on its own guiderails. The combined weight of the elevator car and the counterweight presses the cables into the grooves on the drive sheave, providing the necessary traction as the sheave turns. The weight of the car is balanced by this counterweight. The counterweight weighs about the weight of the car when it is filled to its 40 percent capacity. By keeping the counterweights, the elevator conserves energy, by building up potential energy; effectively the motor takes less power.

When the motor turns in one direction, the pulley raises the elevator; when it turns in the other direction, the pulley lowers the elevator. Both the car and the counterweight travel on guide rails along the sides of the elevator shaft. The rails actually guide the car and counterweight from swaying back and forth; in addition, they also guide the safety governor mechanism to stop the car in an emergency.

70 Roman architect Vitruvius reported that Archimedes built his first elevator probably in 236 BC. The first screw drive elevator was built and installed by Ivan Kulibin in Winter Palace in 1793. Henry Waterman of New York is credited with inventing the 'standing rope control' for an elevator in 1850. In 1852, Elisha Otis introduced the safety elevator, which prevented the fall of the cab if the cable broke. The design is still used today.

An electrically operated brake between the motor and the gear reducer stops the elevator almost instantaneously, at the desired floor level. These elevators typically operate at speeds 500 feet per minute (3 m/s) and can carry loads even up to a few tons.

Now, what happens if the cable wire breaks? Will the elevator go tumbling down? [71] A governor mechanism holds the car in its place in case of such an eventuality. A powerful clamp clutches the steel governor cable, which activates two safety clamps located beneath the car. Moveable steel jaws wedge themselves against the guiderails until sufficient force is exerted to bring the car to a smooth stop.

Machine Room-less (MRL) Elevators: In this design, the machine room is dispensed with as most of the components are within the elevator shaft. It is similar in all respects except that the machinery is in the lift shaft. The benefits are: more usable space, use less energy, slightly lower cost than other elevators.

Observation Elevator: Glass-walled elevators allow passengers to view the cityscape or the building's beauty or shopping lines as they travel as they travel up and down.

Double-deck Elevator: Double-deck elevators can be seen in high-occupancy buildings and shopping malls. By mounting one car upon another time and space are saved. One car stops at even floors and the other stops at the odd floors. Sometimes two elevators are built so that their cars always move synchronously in opposite directions, and are each other's counterweight.

Freight Elevators: These elevators are specially constructed to withstand the rigors of heavy loads.

Hydraulic Elevators: Car or cabin is still the same. Instead of lifting wire ropes on top a typical hydraulic elevator is pushed by a piston. Piston travels inside a cylinder powered by high pressure hydraulic oil. An electric motor pumps oil into the cylinder. A set of valves control the flow of oil in and out of the cylinder to accomplish a gentle lift or smooth descent of the elevator cabin. Electrical valves control the release of the oil for a gentle. Older elevators required a deep hole to locate long cylinder but presently the elevator shafts are not so deep because of telescopic cylinders used. These elevators are less energy efficient.

Elevator Control: Automatic elevators began to appear as early as the 1930s. Relay-controlled elevator systems remained common until the 1980s.Microprocessor controlled systems have taken their place, which are now the industry standard. The elevators have several sensors to control and protect it and its inmates. While there are many other features the following are the standard.

71 Elisha Graves Otis was born in 1811 in Halifax, Vermont. In 1852, his employer, Bedstead Manufacturing Company asked him to design a freight elevator but soon the company became bankrupt. On September 20, 1853, Otis opened his own shop in part of the bankrupt Bedstead plant. In order to promote his new venture, Otis decided to stage a dramatic demonstration of his new safety elevator at the Crystal Palace Exposition in New York. Otis constructed a complete safety elevator and got it fully loaded with freight. As the crowd gathered, he climbed on board and ordered the platform raised to a height. In full view of the crowd, he cut the hoisting rope with an axe. The crowd gasped. Otis reassured the startled crowd with the cry, 'All safe, gentlemen. All safe.' As he was saying this, the platform stopped where it was as the safety spring locked the lift in position.

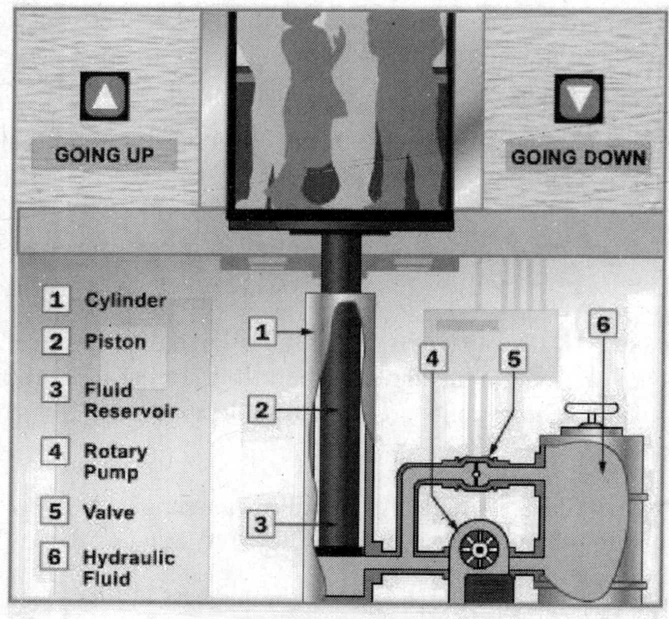

Hydraulic elevator

Elevator Doors: There are always two doors, one at the entry and one door on the moving cabin. If the elevator is not at the designated door, internal locks hold the door from opening. Elevator doors protect riders from falling into the shaft. On the lift itself the most common configuration is to have two panels that meet in the middle, which slide open laterally. Automatic doors close after pre-set time. Doors cannot be opened unless the elevator has reached the designated floor. Sliding and collapsible doors are also common.

Call Buttons: Call buttons to choose a floor are fixed on the floor near the lift and also inside it. Elevators are typically controlled by up and down buttons at each floor stop from the outside or by similar buttons inside panel. But Elevator decides where to stop by a simple algorithm as follows:

When pressed from a certain floor, the elevator arrives to pick up more passengers. If the particular elevator is currently serving traffic in a certain direction, it will only answer all calls in the same direction. This system prevents the lift from going up and down and haywire. In a group of two or more elevators, the call buttons may be linked to ensure that only one car takes precedence.

Special Facilities: A typical modern passenger elevator may also have Security camera, mirrored walls or Glass windows with a view to the building interior or the streets. It may have electric fans or air conditioning to enhance circulation and comfort. An alarm switch is a welcome addition, which passengers can use to alert outsiders that they have been trapped in the elevator. Similarly a telephone is placed inside which can be used by a trapped passenger to call for help or call another phone. Hold and close buttons are normal in most automatic elevators; In automatic door closures, hold button delays the door closing time, useful for last minute entries or loading freight and hospital beds. Close button closes the door without delay.

Floor indicators (LED) and direction lights are standard feature. Direction indicators are found both inside and outside elevator cars which tell you whether the lift is going up or down, In addition, some elevators have a chime to indicate if the elevator is going up or down. Voice prompts are the latest feature in most of the modern elevators which tell when a particular floor is reached. Many elevator installations now feature emergency power systems which allow elevator use in blackout situations and prevent people from becoming trapped in elevators.

Overload sensors are built into modern elevator which prevent the elevator from moving until excess load has been removed

Care and Tips

- ✓ Press only the UP or DOWN button. This is the quickest way of getting an elevator to arrive.
- ✓ When elevator doors start closing, stand clear of them. In grilled elevators keep clear of all the openings. Be extra careful with children.
- ✓ Most of the modern elevators do not move if they are overcrowded. As soon as the overload is removed, the elevator will resume normal operation.
- ✓ If the elevator does not align exactly with the floor of the landing, step over the gap to avoid tripping.
- ✓ If the elevator stops between landings, stay calm. Press the alarm button and wait for instructions from the rescue personnel. In case of such an eventuality, lift doors can be opened from outside by reaching the internal latches with special techniques.
- ✓ If there is a fire or possibility thereof, do not use elevators. Use the staircase.

Domestic Pumps -centrifugal Pump

Water is the life in nature. It is also the force behind the development of every civilisation - in the forest or desert, in the riverside and in the concrete jungles around the world. Domestic pumps are used extensively across the world to lift and/or transport water for personal use, building services, agriculture, industries and a number of other purposes. And they do it efficiently, economically and reliably. Most common pump used is the straight and simple centrifugal pump. Next in the order is the jet pump, submersible pump, piston pump and so on.

Centrifugal Pump: The only moving part in a centrifugal pump is an impeller [72] attached to a shaft which runs inside a casing. Shaft is driven by an electric motor. The impeller can be of cast iron, bronze, stainless steel, or plastic. Casing has suction (inlet) and discharge (outlet) nozzles and facility for the entry of shaft, etc.

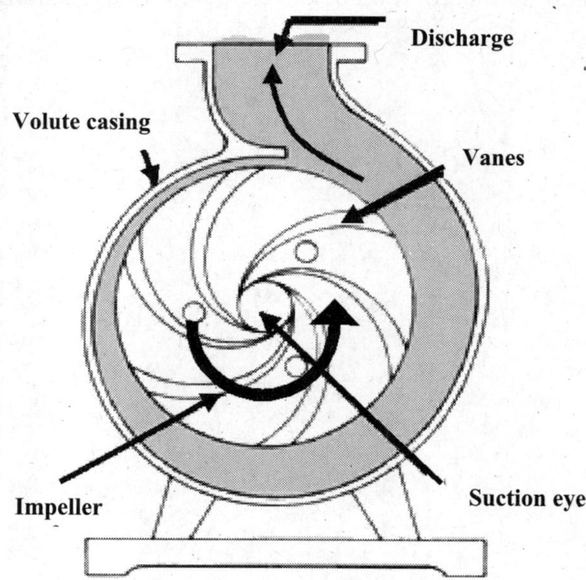

Liquid enters through the inlet to the eye or centre of the impeller where it is rapidly rotated by the impeller blades. Due to the centrifugal force so developed, the liquid is forced outwards and away from the centre with considerable velocity and pressure. The casing with an increasing area closely

72 Probably Denis Papin, created the first centrifugal pump which of course consisted of straight vanes. John Appold developed a curved vane centrifugal pump in 1851.

surrounds the impeller. The casing converts this velocity energy of liquid into additional pressure energy and directs it outside. Further piping leads the water to the point of use. As water leaves the eye of the impeller a low pressure area is created there. Hence, more and more liquid enters the eye as the atmospheric pressure pushes it in.

What Is This Centrifugal Force?: Centrifugal force is the force exerted away from the centre due to rotation. You must have played with bucket of water tied to a rope. If not, play it now! Tie a meter long rope to a small plastic bucket. Fill the bucket with water. Take the end of the rope in your hand and rotate the bucket as fast as you can. You will notice that the water does not spill out of the bucket. That's the centrifugal force preventing water from falling out.

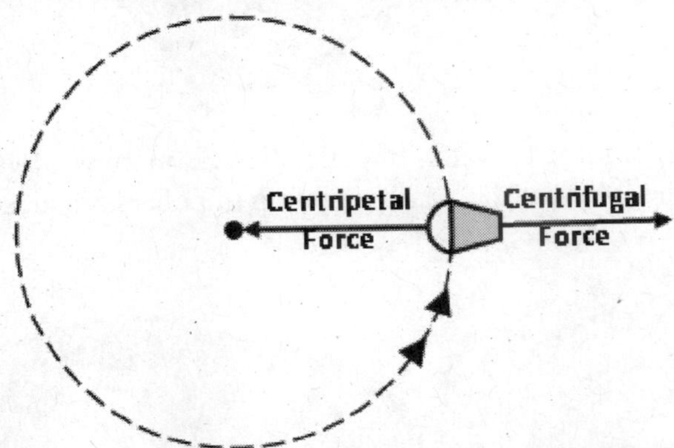

Now if a hole is made in the bottom of the bucket, a jet of water will flow out as the bucket is rotated. That's the centrifugal force throwing the water out. Now, if water can be fed continuously through your arm and the rope, stream of water will be thrown out continuously. There you have the centrifugal pump, most widely used single machine world over. But please note that it is the Mother Nature which is pushing the water in. Our atmosphere exerts a pressure of 14.7 psi or about 1.03 kg/cm^2 all around us at sea level, that's a water column of 33.9 feet high. We have seen that the atmospheric pressure is pushing water into the pump. That limits the suction depth of centrifugal pumps to 33.9 feet or 10.3 meters. In practice, the suction depth is limited to about 23 feet or about 7 meters considering the friction and line losses, which means that you cannot lift water if the depth is more than 7 meters. You must have seen in the past the entire pump was lowered down into the wells, to bring the suction line within those 7 meters. That was before the advent of jet pumps or submersible pumps, better methods to bring water from deeper wells.

Centrifugal pumps have little or no ability to pump air. So, before starting the pump, suction line should be full of water and no air. It is called 'priming of the pump.' Also an air leak in the suction line will make the pump to stop pumping, in other words it 'loses its prime.'

Capacity and Head: Capacity is given in litres per minute. The height to which it can lift water is known as discharge head, in metres and the corresponding pressure is read off a pressure gage mounted on the discharge. Actual head available depends on the line size, restrictions like valves and fittings like elbows and tees, etc.

Parts: Basic parts of a pump are impeller, casing and shaft, while additional parts like gland packing, bearings, housings, coupling play a vital role in making the pump operate smoothly, and leak free.

Impeller- Imparts centrifugal force to water. Impellers have a number of vanes in curved fashion, either in open or closed type. Most of the domestic pump impellers are closed impellers.

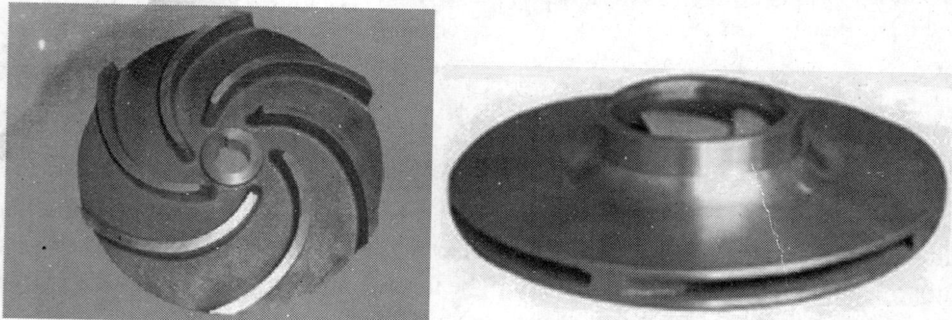

Casing- Encloses the impeller and the liquid, develops the discharge pressure and makes the pump run efficiently.

Shaft- Takes the power from the motor and gives it to the impeller and makes it rotate. It also holds the seals, gland packing, bearings, etc.

Gland packing- There is a small opening in the casing where the shaft enters. Water can leak out of it into atmosphere. So to seal the liquid here from going out, either a gland packing or mechanical seal are used.

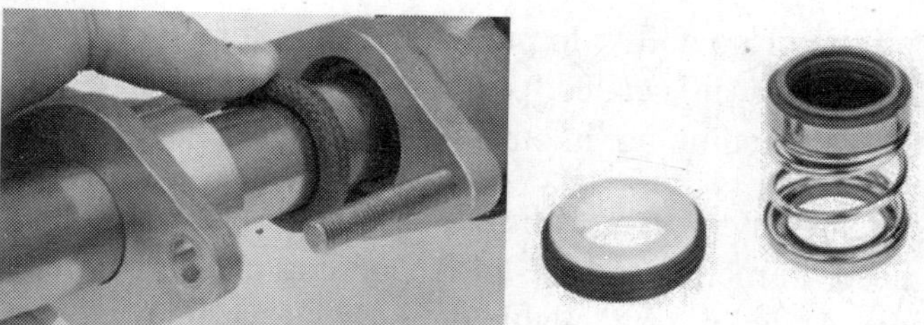

Bearings- Normally, two bearings support the shaft and make it run friction free. Presently most of the pumps use ball bearings; often they are permanently lubricated and sealed.

Bearing Housing- It locates the bearings and also carries oil or grease to lubricate the bearings to reduce friction.

Coupling- Connects the pump to the motor. In smaller pumps, called mono-block pumps, moors directly drive the impeller without the need for the coupling.

Foot Valve- We have read that the pump casing should be always full with water. So, we have to fill the pipe line full before starting the pump. At the end of the suction line one way valve is fixed. This valve will prevent the water from running back into the well. This valve is known as foot valve which is fixed at the end of the suction line.

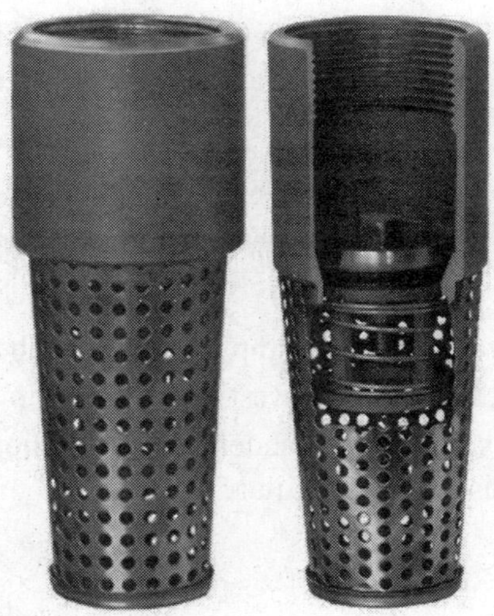

Motor- Most centrifugal pumps are rotated by electric motors operating in the range of 1450 to 3000 rpm. Motors are rated at horse power and normal domestic pumps are ½ HP to 1 HP.

Selection of a Pump: Capacity Needed: To determine the size of the pump, first we need to know how much water in litres per minute are needed. That decides the capacity of the pump. Do not be ambitious and buy a higher capacity pump than your demand or the well can yield.

Well Conditions: We should know how deep the well and what its yield is. Basing on the well depth we can select the pump type, whether it is simple centrifugal pump, jet or bore well pump.

Well yield also will tell us how much water we can draw from it in certain time; thereby decide the capacity of the pump.

Discharge Conditions: Often the pump lifts to an overhead tank. That decides the height up to which the water should be lifted up. Add to it, the route of the piping and the line loss. This decides the discharge head or height.

The above three factors decide the motor power in horse power or kilowatt. Smaller ½ HP pumps are available in single phase. 1 HP pumps are available in one or three phase. Higher power pumps are invariably in three phase.

Select the pump as per your need and power available.

Care and Tips: Domestic pumps last very long when used properly. These small tips help in improving its life

- ✓ Properly size the pump. Oversized capacity pump may deplete the yield of the well.
- ✓ Never run the pump dry, i.e. without water. Surest cause of pump failure is a dry pump.
- ✓ Noisy pump most often indicates the pump is undergoing cavitations i.e., the pump is not getting enough water to pump. Sure cause of pump failure.
- ✓ Lubricate the pump bearings.
- ✓ Make shortest route for suction piping.
- ✓ Avoid unnecessary bends and fittings in the discharge piping.
- ✓ Operate the pump at the recommended voltage and amperage. It is not wise to operate it without its starter and circuit breaker.

Domestic Pumps - Jet Pump

We have seen that normal centrifugal pumps cannot lift water from wells deeper than 7 meters. We are also aware that ground water levels are continuously falling and with the development of more and more multi-storeyed complexes, the necessity for taking out water from the greater depths has become inevitable. Surprisingly, we can still pump water from greater depths with a jet pump or submersible pump. Depth is no longer the limit. Let us look at the jet pumps though they are being taken over by submersible pumps.

Deeper and Deeper: Jet pump is a centrifugal pump with the addition of a jet ejector. Ejector is a very interesting device, extensively used in the industry to create vacuum. They are based on the ejector-venturi principle. An ejector has two inlets: one to admit the motive fluid, now it is water (inlet 1), and the other to inlet deep well water to be pumped (inlet 2). In operation, as the water from inlet 1 travels through an expanding nozzle, its pressure energy converted to velocity energy or the speed of the water is greatly increased, but the pressure drops. You will notice similar action when you pinch the garden hose, water squirts ahead. As the pressure drops, vacuum is created. Due to the suction created, deep well water is sucked in from the inlet 2, and the mixture of fresh and old water enters the venturi diffuser. Here the velocity energy is converted into pressure and the water is let out. In the process water reaches the pumping height and the centrifugal pump takes over again. Part of the discharge water from the pump is again routed back to the injector in the well and the process repeats. In effect some of the water discharged by the impeller passes out of the pump and into the tank.

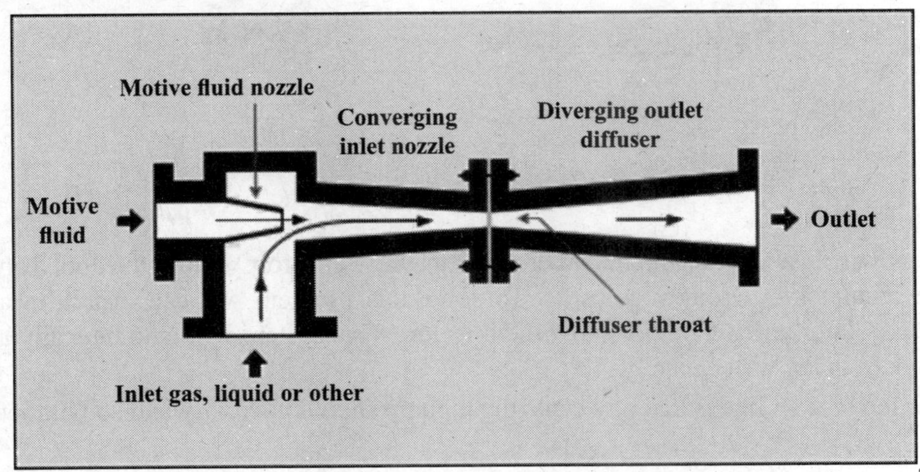

The ejector nozzle and venturi tube size must be properly selected depending on the pumping depth, the size of the pump and the distance of the pump from the well. Because certain amount of water is recirculated in jet pump systems, it is important that the proper sizes of suction and drive lines are used to maximize efficiency. Discharge pressure is also regulated so that the motive water reaches the venturi in the well at sufficient pressure.

Operation: In a typical jet pump installation, there are two pipelines going down the well. One is the suction pipe and the other is the pressure pipe or the return pipe. Both the pipes are connected to the venturi nozzle or the jet assembly. Bottom of this is the foot valve with strainer. Let us start the pump by priming it.

Fill water in the discharge line through or opening a plug. There is small air cock on the pump. Open it. You can see that the air is expelled out as you fill the lines. When no more air is coming out, if only water is squirting out, it means that the lines are full. Start the pump. Tighten the priming plug or close the priming valve, when water flows continuously under pressure around the priming plug. There is a pressure regulator on the discharge line which permits the return water to go down at appropriate pressure. This is very important for the proper ejection of underground water. Now part of the water goes down under pressure to the jet assembly and picks up more water from the underground and submits it to the main pump. The process continues. Deep well jet pumps can be adapted to wells of various depths and yields.v

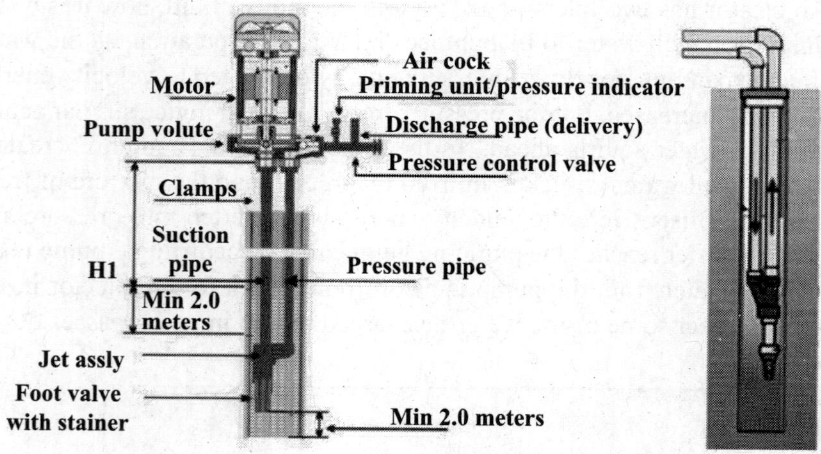

Care and Tips

- ✓ Jet pumps will lose suction if the water level in the well drops below the foot valve or the pressure regulator is wrongly adjusted. To solve this problem, we can install an automatic pressure regulator and a tailpipe below the injector. This system will automatically adjust the pumping rate to the well capacity.
- ✓ However the bottom line is that any centrifugal pump should never dry and so with jet pump.

- ✓ In addition to this, most jet pumps have mechanical seals to prevent leakage across shaft. These are water lubricated and water cooled and hence the pump should never be run dry.
- ✓ Silt, sand, algae and other contaminants can shorten the pump's life. Abrasives particles like sand will wear out the impeller and damage the mechanical seal. Never remove the strainer under the foot valve.
- ✓ Sometimes, particularly on new installations, the nozzle may become partially or completely plugged with dirt or mineral deposits. Then the pump may lose its suction, lose capacity, etc. You may have to lift up the jet assembly. It is a laborious job, which requires professional help.

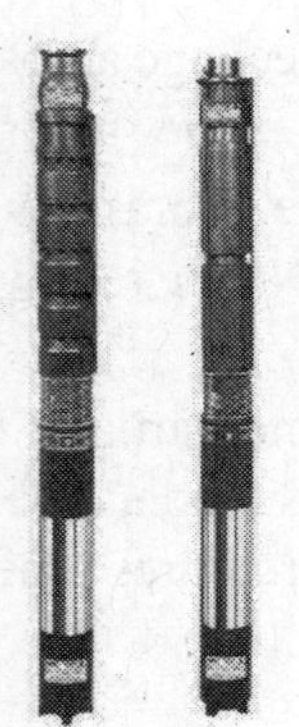

Submersible Pump

No doubt jet pumps have broken the depth barrier of 7 meters impose by centrifugal pumps, they become less efficient as the pumping depth increases. In case of a problem, removal of both pipes and venturi assembly is a tough task. As the technology improved, particularly with the motors, submersible pumps have now become common place. Now instead of lifting the water, we will push it up. Keep the pump in the water and we have the submersible pump.

The submersible pump is a centrifugal pump; as a matter of fact, multiple pumps. Several impellers and casings (stages) are mounted one above the other on a single shaft. Motor is connected to the shaft and is held down below. Discharge is taken up from the final impeller and there is no suction line like ordinary centrifugal pump. There is no recirculation line or drive water as with jet pumps. Several stages of the pump end (wet end) and the motor are joined and submerged in the water.

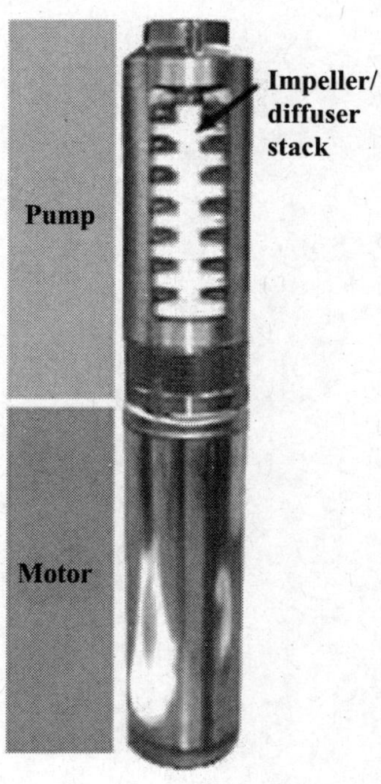

Multi Stage: Practically all submersibles are 'multi-stage' pumps. Each impeller passes the water to the eye of the next impeller through a diffuser. The diffuser converts velocity of water coming right out of the impeller to pressure. A set of impeller and its diffuser is called a stage. As the water is pumped from one impeller to the next, its pressure is increased. Depth from which water is taken out and the height to which it is lifted up decide the number of stages.

A typical submersible pump looks like a long cylinder. The bottom half is made up of a sealed motor. Top half is the pumping unit with series of impellers and diffusers. Well is not the old world open type with a large opening but a bore well of 150 mm or 200 mm diameter and tens of meters deep. A casing pipe is inserted that fits inside the borewell. Total assembly consisting of motor and the pump is lowered down into water in the well. Motor goes down first along with its cables. Naturally, discharge is taken from the top stage by connecting suitable piping. So, the pump is always filled with water or primed and ready to pump. The assembly operates more quietly as it is under water and there is no gland leakage. There is no suction pipe or foot valve, no more fighting gravity and atmospheric pressure. But strainer is necessary to prevent dirt and foreign particles entering the pump. Strainer is suitable mesh wound around the pump casing before the first impeller.

We can stack as many impellers as we need depending on the discharge head required as each impeller increases the pressure by a certain amount. To get more flow we may have to increase the size of the pump or the impeller diameter; in both cases the horsepower of the motor increases. So consider all these factors before buying a pump. Think of also the yield and replenishment of the well before deciding the depth of the borewell.

Submersible pumps are more efficient than jet pumps in delivering water for the same size motor, pump. Submersibles are reliable and often outperform their life for 20 to 25 years without servicing. But in case of problem, it will be necessary to pull out the pump assembly from the well casing; its professional job and a lot of botheration. So, do not compromise on the quality of cables, starters and or piping.